THESE FRAGMENTS
I HAVE SHORED
AGAINST MY RUIN

THESE FRAGMENTS
I HAVE SHORED
AGAINST MY RUIN

CAVEH ZAHEDI

Sticking Place Books
New York

I would like to thank the publications in which
these essays first appeared for their kind permission
to reprint the material here.

Cover design by Teddy Blanks
Cover image © Saul Bromberger & Sandra Hoover Photography

www.stickingplacebooks.com

ISBN 979-8-89976-000-6

CONTENTS

INTRODUCTION

Gilles Deleuze once wrote that most people try to write a bit above their actual level, whereas he tries to write a bit below his. Reading this freed me up: "You mean, I don't have to pretend to be a better writer than I am?"

I have never felt confident in my writing ability. I have also never felt confident in my dancing ability, my body, or my looks. But I like to dance and the truth is that I also like to write, at least when I'm not stressing out about how bad everything I write is, how I can never hope to compete with the great writers of the past, and how everyone who reads this is going to know that I'm a fraud.

This is just to say that I came to writing relatively late in life. I had some self-esteem issues I needed to work through before I could accept that my writing was good enough and that it didn't have to be better than anyone else's.

My friend Tom Adelman (aka Camden Joy) inspired me to write the first piece in this collection. I had been a huge fan of his work and, when he asked me if I would contribute something to a collection of pieces he was putting together about the CMJ Festival (*Dear CMJ, we left the coliseum disappointed...*), I agreed—not because I had any confidence in my ability to write something worth reading—I didn't—but because I was so impressed by his writing style that I thought that if I just imitated it, I couldn't go wrong.

So that's what I did. I wrote a pastiche in his otherwise inimitable style. But I liked how it came out and that gave me the confidence to try again. The second piece in this collection was, I think, rejected by whoever it was who had initially expressed interest in publishing it— I can no longer remember the circumstances of its (still) birth.

Most of the pieces in this collection were written because I needed money and would rather write for money than get a real job. So I owe a debt of gratitude to the editors of the various publications who asked me to write something for them or, more likely, accepted my unsolicited offer to write something for them. Without their kindness and/or gullibility, this volume would not exist.

But the person most responsible for this volume is Paul Cronin. He did not recoil at my suggestion of collecting these sporadic texts into an actual book, as if I were a legitimate filmmaker with something of value to say. If you hate this book, blame him. He could have said, "No, thank you" when he had the chance and spared you, the reader, from the indignity of reading these stray texts written over a span of almost 30 years.

1
I LOVE KATH BLOOM
WITH PLATONIC LOVE

I'm not saying Kath Bloom is the greatest musician that ever lived. She's not (Bach was better). I'm not saying she's the greatest guitar player that ever lived. She's not (Beethoven was better). But I am saying that she's the most soulful singer/songwriter that ever lived. That's right. More soulful than Al Green. More soulful than Morrissey. More soulful even than Karen Peris. So why isn't she more famous? Why isn't she more famous than Al Green, Morrissey, or Karen Peris?

I'll tell you why. Because she's too good. She's so soulful that most people can't take it. Because to be able to appreciate Kath Bloom, one has to have a modicum of soulfulness oneself. And most people sold their souls a long time ago.

And yet, Kath Bloom is not wholly without fame (although she is wholly without money). One of her songs was played on the radio in Los Angeles by DJ Tom Schnabel. But why only one? I went to see Tom Schnabel and brought him a whole tape of songs by Kath Bloom. But did he play any of them? No! Why not? Because Tom Schnabel lacks soul.

I then sent a tape of Kath Bloom songs to DJ Deirdre O'Donaghue, who says she always listens to new material and encourages submissions. Did she ever play any of Kath's songs? No! Why not? Because Deirdre O'Donaghue also lacks soul. Did she even listen to the tape? God only knows, because she never even consented to speak to me and to answer my simple question: have you heard the tape? Instead, she told her volunteer flunkies to tell me she was in a meeting. Well, Deirdre O'Donaghue is a stupid idiot with shitty taste. The only reason she ever played Hugo Largo was because Brian Eno told her he liked them. Now if Brian Eno told her he liked Kath Bloom, she would have played her. But Brian Eno has never heard of Kath Bloom, because she has too much soul.

The only person with the soulful intelligence to play Kath Bloom was filmmaker Rick Linklater, in his (excellent) film *Before Sunrise*. He not only played her, he played her diagetically. Because Rick Linklater has a soul.

And if only you could hear Kath Bloom sing one of her songs, you too would swoon and weep as I do, but to do that you have to have a soul. So if you have no soul, go out and get one and then listen to Kath Bloom. When that happens, we will all swoon and weep together, instead of separately and alone.

—From The CMJoy Gang

Published in the pamphlet *Dear CMJ, we left the coliseum discouraged…: Posters of Protest from the CMJoy Gang*, 1999

2
SIGNS FROM GOD

On September 17, 1999, my friend Greg Watkins and I flew to New York from San Francisco to attend the Independent Feature Film Market where *A Sign From God*, a 35 mm feature that Greg had written and directed (and which I had acted in, co-produced, and edited) was scheduled to screen in the "Rough Cuts" section. We had come to the Market because we needed finishing funds to complete the film and were hoping to generate enough "buzz" about the film to attract finishing money. It was my third time at the market. I had already been there in 1990 with *A Little Stiff* (which Greg and I had co-directed), and in 1994 with *I Don't Hate Las Vegas Anymore*.

Saturday, September 18
9:00am
We arrive at the registration desk. The pretty woman who hands us our materials is pretty unfriendly. When I ask her what we're supposed to do next, she answers "whatever you want," as if the question were idiotic beyond belief. She also hands us an ugly tote bag with an ugly *Time Out* logo emblazoned on it. It is crammed with all kinds of useless stuff (t-shirts, baseball hats, rulers, each of them an advertisement for something or other) that we now have to carry around town.

9:30am

We run into Michelle Byrd, the director of the market, in line at the Angelika cafe counter. She, unlike the woman at the registration desk, is the epitome of politeness, but in a no-nonsense way that I find refreshing. At the moment, she is a bit frustrated by the fact that her scone doesn't look very fresh, and regrets not having gotten breakfast before coming here. I am approached by another film-maker who recognizes me from *Citizen Ruth* and has actually memorized my one crappy line. He delivers it much better than I did. I realize that this is Phillip B. Roth, the director of *I Was a Jewish Sex Worker*.

12:00pm

I'm at the Fox Searchlight "Meet the Buyers" panel. I'm getting that sinking feeling again of powerlessness and of insignificance. Listening to the collective discourse, I'm finding myself falling prey to the feeling of wanting to be one of the people they're talking about, which is some-thing I've been relatively immune to ever since I left L.A. a year ago and moved to San Francisco. But here, given the consensus-reality of success and big-budget produc-tion, Michael Hoffman (the director of *A Midsummer Night's Dream*) suddenly seems like someone to emulate. Once again I wonder what I'm doing here. Greg tells me he's getting depressed too.

1:30pm

Still looking for a place to spend the night. My lack of accommodations accentuates my feeling of being adrift in a hostile environment. Maybe I should just give in and get a hotel room. I just really can't afford it. But maybe I shouldn't let that stop me. I don't know what to do.

3:30pm
The indie distributors film panel just ended. That was pretty depressing too. I don't know who I am anymore. I'm losing my sense of identity pretty fast.

4:00pm
I need a break. I'm going to go sit outside in the sun while Greg watches a work-in-progress screening about shamanism.

5:30pm
Sitting on the sidewalk outside the public theater, Cain Devore walks by. He tells us that Jeff Dowd, the famous producer's rep (whom we've never heard of), has agreed to rep his film. Greg and I start to feel that we should maybe get a producer's rep too.

6:00pm
Thank God there's no party tonight.

8:00pm
Moe, one of our private investors, flies into town from L.A. His companion missed her plane, so Moe puts me up for the night.

Sunday, September 19
10:00am
Woke up late. Once again I won't have time to meditate before rushing out into the world.

10:49am
Sitting in the cab on my way to Lisa's to pick up her key (I'm staying at her place tonight), I'm starting to feel much better. Life seems much more pleasant from inside a taxi cab.

12:22pm
I've just attended the "Meet the Buyers" series featuring David Koh of Winstar. He seems to be a nice guy but I continue to be appalled by the vulgar self-promotionalism with which my fellow filmmakers preface each of their questions. I feel embarrassed to be one of them.

12:42pm
Greg and I walk up to David Koh and introduce ourselves. I'm assuming he'll recognize us but he doesn't. I tell him who we are but he's never heard of us. We hand him a card with the info about our screening. He says he'll try to see the film in the tape library. I explain to him that we need $30,000 to finish it. He nods blankly.

2:00pm
I can't decide whether I should catch the tail end of the "Art of Editing" panel or if I should sit outside in the sun and try to meditate a little bit. I end up checking out the "Art of Editing" panel.

2:30pm
I run into Phillip B. Roth again outside the Public Theater. He explains to me that tomorrow is Yom Kippur and not to be surprised if nobody shows up to our screening.

5:00pm
In the middle of our networking meeting with Lifesize Entertainment. I spot the great Iranian film director, Amir Naderi, outside the window looking in. He recognizes me, waves, and walks in to greet me. I excuse myself from the meeting and go to greet him. I am grateful for this opportunity to make an exit.

5:45pm
Greg and I have tea with Cauleen Smith. She tells us all about her producer's rep, Neil Friedman, and offers to talk to him about our project.

7:00pm
Moe suggests I shoot a film in Iran. He claims it will put me on the map. I assume he means the Iranian map.

Monday, September 20
11:00am
Woke up pretty late again. Still on West Coast time.

12:30pm
There are about five people at our screening. Normally I'd be freaking out, but I've lowered my expectations so much over the years that I just think it's kind of funny.

12:35pm
There are now about 25 people in the audience. But in 1990 when *A Little Stiff* premiered and I was a total unknown, I could swear there were about 100 people. Either people know better than to come see our movies now or times have changed.

2:19pm
The screening has ended. It was nice to hear everybody laughing during the screening and I guess all the walk-outs were to be expected. Afterwards, the only people who approach us (beside other filmmakers who liked it) are Lynda Hansen and Christoph Terhechte from the Berlin Film Festival. Christoph tells us he liked the film and encourages us to submit it to Berlin, but is concerned about it being finished in time. I explain the situation to him and he offers us a one month extension on the Berlin deadline.

3:00pm
Just had tea and apple crumb cake with Bob Hawk. He gives us his notes on the film (which I dutifully write down) and suggests we make further cuts before submitting it to Sundance. I explain to him that our only hope of getting finishing funds is to get accepted to Sundance but he tells us that getting into Berlin should probably get us finishing funds as well.

5:30pm
Just got out of the digital filmmaking panel. Not much I didn't know, but it was inspiring nonetheless. In the lobby, the filmmakers around me are darting anxious glances at every potential buyer or distributor. It's almost impossible for an authentic and non-manipulative human interaction to occur in such an environment. It makes me want to work only in digital.

6:00pm
Outside the Public Theater, I notice Scott Macaulay trying to get away from the crowd. He is stopped by a desperate-looking filmmaker who corners him. I see other filmmakers starting to notice him standing there and zeroing in on him like sharks around a bleeding fish. Before long, an increasingly large circle of filmmakers has formed around him, hemming him in. I'm glad I'm not him.

6:30pm
The "Market Madness" party is too crowded to even move through. I don't see Greg so I go outside. It's good to be out in the open air. I sit on the stoop waiting for Greg to show up so we can get the hell out of here. Under other circumstances, I'd be interested in meeting these filmmakers, but given the fact that everyone here is trying to sell something, I feel no desire to take part in the general frenzy.

7:15pm
Some guy on the street walks up to me and asks if I was the guy in *A Sign From God*. He tells me I was very funny and asks me how far along the film is. I tell him we still need approximately $30,000 in finishing funds. I get the impression that he thinks I think he might be a potential investor. He leaves abruptly.

7:30pm
Greg finally arrives. He's pretty depressed about the screening.

7:45pm
Lisa invites us to a Producer's party. There are no invitations for this one. You just have to know about it, and now we know. But Greg and I decide to have dinner instead. He's going back to San Francisco tomorrow.

Tuesday, September 21
9:30am
Woke up late again, as usual. It's raining, and the last thing I feel like doing is rushing over to the Angelika to maximize schmoozing time.

9:45am
I accidentally brush my teeth with diaper rash ointment.

1:50pm
It's raining and I accidentally step in a huge puddle. My shoes are soaked.

2:30pm
Moe and I leave the panel on script development after a half hour. I vow not to go to any more panels.

3:00pm
I pick up the mail from our mailbox. It's mostly just
junk mail from other filmmakers but I do find the list
of who came to our screening. I'm amazed by who's on
it. Miramax, Artisan, the Independent Film Channel,
Seventh Arts. I had no idea.

3:30pm
Moe and I find a place to sit right by the entrance of the
Angelika lobby. I'm amazed by the number of people
who keep walking up to me. This is definitely the place
to be. Cooper from the Sundance Film Festival walks up
to me and tells me he's heard good things about *A Sign
From God*. I immediately start to enumerate all the flaws
in the movie. Cauleen tries to do some damage control
by pointing out what a harsh critic I am. Cooper concurs
that "Caveh is very picky." I tell him about my 1999
video diary and my plans to submit it to Sundance before
it's finished. He says that's fine. I am relieved and a little
less depressed.

5:30pm
This is definitely the place to sit. I'm having the best time
I've had at the market just sitting here. I feel like Lao Tse.

6:00pm
The Angelika is closing, so we decide to go to the cocktail party being hosted by some filmmakers. They've
bought drinks for everybody. I wonder how much this
cost them.

Wednesday, September 22
10:00am
Woke up late again. I just hope this doesn't happen
tomorrow. I have to be at the screening at 9:30 am.

11:00am
Melody London calls and asks if I can speak to her NYU class today at 4:00 pm.

3:45pm.
I pick up the tape from the video library to show to Melody's class. A buyer tells me he was planning to watch it later this afternoon. Bummer.

5:00pm
I run into Amy Taubin from *The Village Voice*. She tells me she saw the movie and was loving it until the last twenty minutes. She says she spoke to Simon Field of the Rotterdam Film Festival and that he said the same exact thing.

5:15pm
We check our mailbox and find a list of the people who have watched our film at the video library. There are only seven names on it.

6:00pm
I have tea with Amin Naderi, who accidentally spills his coffee all over my clothes.

Thursday, September 23
7:30am
Harris wakes me up. Thank God.

8:00am
The longer I attend the market, the more I realize that the IFP path is not mine. This is not the way I would like to live my life, and this is not the way I would like to go about making films.

11:00am
Our film ends. There weren't a lot of people in the theater, so there weren't as many laughs as at our first screening. Michael Kastenbaum waxes effusive, as do a couple of other people. I've been so down on the film and told everybody how flawed it is that everyone is surprised by how good it actually is.

3:40pm
Just finished interviewing my friend Keith for my Portrait film. I'm waiting for the F train to arrive. It looks like I may be late for my 4:00 pm networking meeting.

4:05pm
I'm late for my 4:00 pm networking meeting. I wonder if I should just forget the whole thing. I'm not sure why exactly I'm meeting with someone from Sony Pictures Classics, except that one day I may be doing business with this person and will know more about them, but it seems like a pretty silly reason to be rushing to this meeting weighted down by my tripod and camera.

4:50pm
The networking meeting was actually quite enjoyable. The Sony Pictures Classics representative was likeable, intelligent and down to earth and my peers were not too vulgar in their attempts to impress her. One guy tells her that his film has already been accepted by Sundance. She seems impressed. I feel envious.

5:15pm
I walk with Zeinabu Davis from Broome Street to the Angelika. She explains to me that her film took seven years to complete. I am stunned.

6:30pm
I meet with Jason Kliot of Open City Films. I tell him about the video diary, which he seems to like the idea of, and we discuss the possibility of his providing finishing funds for it. This is actually the most constructive thing to have come out of my trip to New York.

Friday, September 24
6:00am
I wake up full of energy for some reason, unable to sleep.

8:00am
I notice that there's a panel on completion financing happening today at 9:00. Even though I vowed not to go to any more of these panels, I decide to go anyway.

8:50am
I'm on the corner of 4th Avenue and East 11th Street heading towards the Public Theater where a complimentary breakfast supposedly awaits me.

8:55am
No sign of breakfast anywhere. I ask one of the IFFM staff about it and they tell me that the complimentary breakfast is being served at another location, several blocks away.

9:00am
I call Lisa to try to get together before I leave, and she tells me that our film is getting a lot of good "buzz."

9:05am
A fellow filmmaker is handing out hand-made fans with the title of his film printed on them. He is walking up to every person in the room, fanning himself while commenting on the heat (it's not hot at all), and then smilingly offering each person a free fan.

11:15am
Neil Friedman, Cauleen's producer's rep, walks up to me in the lobby of the Angelika. He recognizes me from my acting role in *Money Buys Happiness*, which he is apparently representing. I tell him that Greg and I are looking for a producer's rep for our film as well. He gives me his card and I make a mental note to call him when I get back to San Francisco.

12:30pm
Walking away from the Angelika, I feel a slight pang of nostalgia. As much as I dislike the Market and hate the whole idea of marketing oneself, I suddenly feel an inexplicable sadness at leaving. Could it be that I actually had fun?

Previously unpublished, 1999

3
I IS ANOTHER*

For me, the central question in art is that of the ego. I suppose, for me the central question in life is that of the ego, but for me art and life are one and the same, so I will just talk about art for now.

The medieval view of the artist is one I feel much closer to than the Enlightenment view. In the middle ages, the artist was seen as a humble servant of God, doing God's work to the best of his ability. Starting with the Renaissance, this view gradually started to change. The artist became increasingly self-important as his faith in God increasingly diminished.

The cult of personality replaced the ancient mystical cults, and the artist was increasingly seen as more than human. This cult of personality can be seen in the way we view heroic artist figures such as Michelangelo, Beethoven, and Van Gogh, to name only a few. What we admire in these artists is their individuality, their uniqueness. But I believe that all art is "channeled," i.e. that it comes from God, however one defines that word. But the modern view of art is that it is the self-expression of a sui generis individual, a "genius" who is somehow more brilliant and talented than the rest of us.

---

* The title is a line from Rimbaud ("Je Est Un Autre").

The truth is that we are all manifestations of the genius of God. The artist is no different than anyone else except insofar as he is closer to the source of his Being. But today, the artist has acquired the status of a saint, and the culture of celebrity has become our new religion. Only instead of a panoply of saints, known for their virtue and good works, we have movie stars and rock stars as religious icons. These people are worshipped not because of their spirituality or wisdom, but rather because they enable us to project a more grandiose image of ourselves — namely that, like them, we too can be more important and powerful than we actually feel ourselves to be.

This problem of the ego in art stems in part from the fact that our self-worth has been severely eroded. To compensate for this erosion, artists have tended to emphasize their specialness, and to attempt to make themselves appear better than those around them. This is a big problem for the arts because if all art is in fact "channeled," then Art rests on a connection to the Source of all creation. The problem with the ego in art is that it destroys this connection to the source by positing itself as the source, much like the Satan figure in Milton's *Paradise Lost.*

This temptation is almost inevitable for the artist, as it was for Flaubert's Saint Anthony. But the greatest artists are those who resist this temptation. Rimbaud, who ultimately failed to resist this temptation and so ceased to be an artist before he died, referred to this aspect of art when he compared the artist to an anchorite. So the fundamental question for the artist, as indeed for anyone, is the question of the ego: namely, what to do about the existence of the ego? For the religious person, this question might be posed in the form of: what to do about the existence of the Devil? But I am not a religious person, so I prefer to talk about the ego.

Franz Kafka attempted to answer this question in several ways. One way was to not finish what he started (none of his novels was ever completed). Another way was to not publish what he wrote (most of his writing he never attempted to publish). Finally, he tried to destroy what he had written (he asked, on his death bed, that his friend Max Brod burn all his papers, a request which Max Brod fortunately disobeyed). But none of these strategies was sufficient unto itself, which is why Kafka did finish and publish some stories, and gave Max Brod the impression that he was at least ambivalent about his request to have his papers burned after his death. So what was Kafka doing?

I believe that Kafka was trying to resolve this problem of the ego in art: how does one make art that is not inextricably bound up with ego? And the simple answer is that one can't. Rather, one must engage with the ego in a dialectical and hopefully sly way, because the ego is exceedingly tricky, even if God is still trickier.

Maurice Blanchot, Kafka's spiritual heir and the most insightful commentator on Kafka's spiritual travails, argues that Kafka's strategy was a brilliant one, but that it must be seen holistically to be fully understood. For Blanchot, Kafka's art and life were of a piece and indistinguishable. In this sense, it could be argued that Kafka was the first performance artist, making of his life a work of art, and of his art a kind of exegesis of his life.

Blanchot inherited Kafka's dilemma, and solved the problem for himself in a similar yet radically different way: Blanchot addressed the problem of the ego in art by writing a work, *Thomas the Obscure*, that would pose a central enigma to the reader. The answer to this enigma would be found not in the work itself, but in Blanchot's life.

Blanchot never allowed himself to be photographed. The fact that he never allowed himself to be photographed means that he had no publically recognizable face. The fact that he had no publically recognizable face means that a question is posed by his supremely diffident relationship to publicity, namely: what does Maurice Blanchot look like? This question is echoed in his seminal work, *Thomas the Obscure*, by a related question: who is Thomas the Obscure?

In 1945, when the Nag Hammadi library was discovered in Egypt, *The Gospel of Thomas* was among the texts that were rediscovered. In *The Gospel of Thomas*, Jesus asks his apostles the question: who am I like? According to the Apocrypha, Thomas was Christ's twin brother, and he is the only apostle who guessed the answer to the question, although the answer is never revealed in the text. But the answer is clear: you are like me.

The implications of this answer are far-reaching, and led to the complete annihilation of the Gnostics and of their sacred texts by orthodox Christianity. *The Gospel of Thomas* was one of these sacred texts, and was thought lost until 1945, when it was discovered in Nag Hammadi. The astonishing thing is that Blanchot's *Thomas the Obscure* was published in 1945 as well, having been written immediately before the discovery of the lost *Gospel*. And yet, the lost *Gospel* was the missing piece that provided the answer to the enigma: what does Maurice Blanchot look like?

Blanchot has done an almost inconceivable thing by figuring out how to keep the ego out of the work of art in this way. The fact that he could not have known about the existence of the Nag Hammadi library text when he composed *Thomas the Obscure* can only be explained, it seems to me, by a kind of mystical channeling, or gnosis, on Blanchot's part. In other words, this information could only have been revealed to him.

Such revelation brings us to the question of the ego in cinema. Because the art of cinema requires the photographic reproduction of reality, Blanchot's aston-

ishing solution to the problem is not an option for the
filmmaker. In fact, the opposite strategy is required:
a complex dialectic between celebrity (a quasi-inevita-
bility) and anonymity (almost a spiritual necessity). In
my own work, I have chosen to address this problem by
making films about myself, and by consequently docu-
menting the most intimate details of my private life. At
the same time, I have employed one of the distinguishing
elements of cinema: namely its unique relation to randomness, which one could also call Fate or Reality or God.

Another way of saying this is: how does one
channel God in cinema? For me, the answer has been: by
removing oneself from the equation. In other words: by
surrendering will. But one cannot simply remove oneself
from the equation, nor can one make a film without
exerting will. So what does one do? A complex dialectic
is required, in which will and the surrender of will work
hand in hand, and in which ego and the repudiation of
ego also go hand in hand.

All of my films have been an attempt to bring God
back into the picture, so as to take my own ego out of
the center of the frame. But the ego is a hydra, and keeps
growing back. So how does one slay this self-regener-
ating dragon?

In *I Don't Hate Las Vegas Anymore*, I dispensed
with the script entirely and trusted to chance (a.k.a. God)
to provide the narrative of the film. I also enacted the
dialectical struggle between ego and non-ego (between
will and the surrender of will) by being both actor and
director. These two roles were usually in conflict, but the
embodying of that conflict was the true subject of the film.
The result is a film directed by God, in which the ego self
is not denied, but in which it doesn't have the upper hand
either. It is an instance of God being trickier than the ego.

In *I Was Possessed By God*, the strategy was more
direct and almost scientific. I ingested five grams (an

extremely large dose) of hallucinogenic mushrooms during the making of the film. This obliterated my ego, at least ostensibly and for a few hours, and allowed God to "speak directly" through me. The ego is still there I believe, but it has been put in its place and, at least for a while, is no longer running the show.

With *In the Bathtub of the World*, my goal was to reveal the existence of God in all things. In order to do this, I resorted to randomness once again, and to a deliberate critique of "specialness." The film exploits the most democratic genre that exists, the home movie, in order to reveal the workings of the divine in all of our lives. I had no idea what would happen in the film, but I knew that only a subtle combination of will (demanding of myself that I shoot one minute every day) and surrender (I would try to listen each day to "hear" what I was supposed to do that day) would lead to the result that I desired, namely a film that would also be a work of art, meaning a work that has in some way been channeled.

So who am I in all this? An Other, certainly. But also a specific Other: God. And also Thomas, Christ's twin brother, whose full name is given in the New Testament as "Thomas Judas Didymus," which means twin in three languages (Hebrew, Aramaic, and Greek). And also Christ, the link between God and Man, whom Thomas touches after Christ's death and in so doing finds himself transfigured, understanding that he is thereby touching his own death and that he is connected to his own divinity by death. And also Maurice Blanchot, whose face I have never seen and most likely never will, but which I know to be identical to mine. And also you, "cher lecteur, mon semblable, mon frère."[*]

Infinity Film Festival catalogue, 2001

---

[*] The quote is from, "Au Lecteur," the opening poem of Baudelaire's *Les Fleurs du Mal*.

4
IN THE SHADOW OF THE VAMPIRE

E. Elias Merhige's *Shadow of the Vampire* revisits the set of director F. W. Murnau's 1922 horror classic *Nosferatu* to tell an imagined story of Murnau (John Malkovich) and his obscure star Max Schreck (played brilliantly by Willem Dafoe). Murnau, in order to maximize the film's realism, casts an actual vampire, offering—in exchange for Schreck's willingness to "play himself"—to sacrifice his unsuspecting leading lady in the final scene of the film. Unfortunately, Schreck almost immediately begins indulging his bloodlust on hapless crew members. The central conflict of the film thus revolves around Murnau's increasingly desperate attempts to get his refractory vampire to behave so that he can get his film finished before everyone in the cast and crew is dead. The result of this clever narrative conceit is a film that walks a subtle tightrope between creepiness and hilarity.

In 1991, Merhige directed *Begotten*, a film that Susan Sontag called "one of [the] 10 most important films of modern times." An utterly original work, it nevertheless bears comparison both to *Eraserhead* and the brilliantly surrealist films of Canadian filmmaker Guy Maddin.

Applying many of the principles of the primal Japanese dance movement Butoh, *Begotten* tells the story

of cosmic creation (brought about by God's mastur-
bating) and human birth (most of the film is taken up
with the tortuous process of exiting the womb). It uses
no dialogue whatsoever, and captures a depth of human
experience that is all too rare in American cinema.

After making *Begotten,* Merhige spent much
of the '90s trying to parlay that $33,000 film into a
Hollywood directing deal. He spent years just trying
to get it seen, and after a few showings at festivals and
museums, it was finally released on video in 1996. Rock
star Marilyn Manson, attracted by the video cover,
rented the film one night and was blown away by what
he saw. He tracked Merhige down and asked him to
direct his next music video. Merhige readily agreed,
and his video for Manson's "Anti-Christ Superstar"
was the only film the director managed to make in the
10 years after *Begotten.*

A year later, a friend of Nicolas Cage saw *Begotten*
and showed it to the actor. Cage loved the film, and,
like Manson before him, tracked Merhige down. As
Merhige puts it, "We got together and had a wonderful
meeting and talked about everything from Leonardo
Da Vinci to Nikola Tesla." Three days later, Cage sent
Merhige the script for *Shadow of the Vampire* and
offered to act as executive producer on the film. Merhige
"fell in love with it," and Cage contacted Malkovich
and Dafoe, Merhige's top choices to play the leads.
After meeting with Merhige, both actors agreed to
do the film. The financing came from pre-sales based
on the attached actors, and the film was picked up for
distribution even before Merhige had finished cutting
it. The film was subsequently invited to Cannes, where
it garnered almost universal accolades.

The story of the making of *Shadow of the Vampire*
is one of those indie-filmmaker Cinderella stories, with
Merhige as the dustbin waif struggling in obscurity for

a decade before being plucked out of said obscurity by Nicolas Cage's prince. It is the American Indie dream, and few struggling filmmakers are immune to its allure. But like the Faustian bargain in the film itself between Murnau and his star, there is a price to pay. And that price is an inevitable concession to the demands of the marketplace. For while *Shadow of the Vampire* is a wholly entertaining and engaging film, it ultimately pales in comparison to *Begotten*, a bona fide masterpiece despite its relative obscurity. The unavoidable need to please the producers and to recoup the film's investment has created a work that must out of necessity clothe its more radical ideas in the less threatening guise of allegory rather than embodying them directly. And the allegory of the vampire's ultimate unwillingness to honor the terms of his bargain with Murnau can be seen as a deeply melancholy critique of the always inevitable erosion of art by the forces of the marketplace.

The Stranger, 2001

5
THE STATE OF AMERICAN FILM CRITICISM

> "Critics sometimes appear to be addressing themselves to works other than those I remember writing" —Joyce Carol Oates

Since my film, *I Am A Sex Addict*, opened theatrically on April 5th, it has received a bewildering gamut of reviews, ranging from "it's pure torture" to "it's the most moving, insightful and funny confessional personal journey the movies have given us in a long, long time." The spectrum of responses has been disconcerting.

I started a blog fairly recently, on which I wrote critiques of some of the film reviews I had been getting. I almost immediately got a nervous flurry of posts on my blog, most of them anonymous, complaining about these critiques. The comments ranged from "It's undignified to argue with critics" to "Stop Whining, bitch!" But since when are filmmakers not supposed to respond to their critics? Filmmaking is a form of communication, so why should that communication stop with the film itself?

A lot of people read film reviews. I would argue that there are more film reviews read each year than there are movies watched. People like to read them.

They don't require a long attention span. They don't require a lot of education. And they give the reader the feeling that they are in the know. But because film criticism is so widely read, film critics have an inordinate influence not just on the public's perception of particular films, but also on the public's perceptions in general. Film reviews reveal a tremendous amount about the ideological assumptions of the writers who wrote them, and yet no one seems to be commenting on those ideological assumptions.

If all films have implicit ideologies (and I believe they all do), then so do all film reviews. There are competing ideas about what the problems and solutions are to the world's problems. Film reviewers have just as much responsibility as anyone else to examine their own hidden ideological assumptions and, with humility, open their minds to what they don't yet know. It helps no one for filmmakers to remain silent in the face of nonsense being impressed upon people's minds. Malcolm Gladwell has shown the extent to which human beings are susceptible to suggestion in *The Tipping Point*. Our collective reality is made and remade each day, but it is made of free-floating words and phrases and ideas. And film is one of the most powerful vehicles in the history of art for *ideological warfare*. As filmmakers, we are trying to persuade our fellow human beings to see things a certain way, a different way. So why stop at the movie screen?

The question I would like to explore is: what are the ideological assumptions implicit in contemporary American film criticism? Fortunately for us, there are as many answers to that question as there are critics. But analyzed on a case-by-case basis, certain distressing patterns begin to emerge, and a picture of the underlying ideological assumptions of present-day American society begins to take shape.

What I propose is to pick a review at random and analyze it paragraph by paragraph for its underlying ideological assumptions. The review I have chosen is my most recent film review, and I have chosen it for that reason alone. This review appeared in the *Orlando Sentinel* on June 24th and was written by Roger Moore.

I

Let's begin with the opening paragraph of Mr. Moore's review:

"That self-indulgent documentary form, the biographical essay film, earns its most onanistic installment ever in *I Am a Sex Addict*, the latest from comically self-involved Caveh Zahedi."

The contempt with which he writes: "That self-indulgent form, the biographical essay film" is a contempt that he shares, sadly, with a surprising number of fellow critics ("singularly narcissistic," "egocentric asshole," "He may be the most self-involved person on the face of the Earth," etc.). According to Mr. Moore, biographical essay films are, by definition, "self–indulgent." And he's not the only one who believes that. He's only the most recent in a long line. Other critics who have called my film "self-indulgent" include: Jay Carr (*amNew York*), Carina Chocano (*Los Angeles Times*), James DiGiovanna (*Tucson Weekly*), Steve Erickson (*Gay City News*), Ted Fry (*Seattle Times*), David Poland (his blog), and Nick Schlager (*Slant*).

The taboo against self-reflection or autobiography is, for me, one of the more bewildering hidden ideological assumptions that I have discovered in the course of my film's release. But what does self-indulgence even mean? Mr. Moore has not bothered to ask himself that. In his prose, it is a given. It is not elucidated. It is pejorative, it is magisterial, and that is enough. It is a subtle form of name-calling that one finds to an alarming degree in the various reviews: ("sicko," "asshole," "jerk," etc.).

I would argue that "self-indulgence" is behavior that is unaware and/or insensitive to the other. A self-indulgent filmmaker is a filmmaker who is only interested in pleasing himself and has no care or concern for the viewer's pleasure and/or interest. Such a filmmaker is the kind who would say: "I don't care if nobody at the screening liked it. I liked it, and that's that."

Such a filmmaker is imaginable, but there is nothing about the biographical essay film in general that is self-indulgent. One could make a self-indulgent biographical essay film or a non-self-indulgent biographical essay film, in the same way that one could make a self-indulgent action film or a non-self-indulgent action film. The epithet "self-indulgent" has nothing to do with the genre. It is entirely a question of execution.

II

But let's move on to the next paragraph. Mr. Moore writes:

"Zahedi, a Woody-Allen homely little weasel with a thing for drugs (his *I Was Possessed by God* recounts a vivid mushroom trip), women, and most of all, himself, creates these little pseudo-biographical essays that suggest he's either a spoiled jerk with access to cameras, or a wit whose jerkiness is something of a pose."

Mr. Moore's description of me as "homely" is only the latest instance of a long line of such epithets: ("an unattractive creature who resembles a human bug," "hairless chihuahua," "odd-looking duck," etc.). Granted, I act in my film, and since the film re-enacts my addiction to prostitutes as well as my relationships with some of the women in my life, my attractiveness quotient arguably has some relevance to the story. But the use of the word "weasel" in the context of "homely little weasel" shows Mr. Moore's hand. The word is being used passive-aggressively, and it is meant as a personal attack or, from the point of view of Mr. Moore, as a counter-attack.

The political implications here begin to show. "Homely" implies its opposite, someone who would be the opposite of homely—Brad Pitt, say, or Angelina Jolie. But why is there no reflection on the idea of "homely"? Is there even such a thing? Or is it just a false category that makes us miserable because we buy into it and suffer under its tyranny?

My film is, among other things, a refutation of the dualism implicit in the use of the word "homely." My film is counter-ideological in that sense, if one accepts the premise that there is intense ideological pressure in our society to conform to a certain standard of Beauty. It is a pressure that is causing tremendous unhappiness among millions of perfectly lovely people and which ultimately affects everyone.

There is a beauty war. There are those who insist on maintaining the classical Western standards (which find their highest expression in actors such as Tom Cruise and Nicole Kidman), and there are those who are arguing for a much wider spectrum or, even better, for no dualism at all. Mr. Moore, in this instance, is just cracking a whip that he too has been whipped by, and many times. It is merely another instance of the oppressed identifying with their oppressors.

The words "spoiled jerk" are also indicative. Again, we have the same dualism as before: a person is either a jerk or he's not a jerk. Jerkiness isn't a passing state but a permanent one. It is, in other words, ontological: so and so *is* a jerk. He's not merely *being* jerky. The implication is that he's forever and irremediably a "jerk."

This is the ideology of enemy-making. This is the same ideology that buys into catchphrases like "the axis of evil" and influences people to elect demagogues like George W. Bush. The words "spoiled jerk" sound quintessentially Republican, with all the contempt they imply for social services and for simple Christian charity.

And then there's the Woody Allen reference. The constant reference to Woody Allen by film reviewers only shows the narrowness of their film education. It's as if they have no other literary or artistic references to compare the film to, and can only resort to their one touchstone. They've apparently never seen a film by Godard. If there's a guy talking to the camera, he must be imitating Woody Allen. The ignorance of film history that this shows is, to me, startling.

III

But let's continue:

"He's not as political as Michael Moore (*Roger & Me*), not as charming as Ross McElwee (*Sherman's March*), not as boring as Alan Berliner (*Wide Awake*). Zahedi's niche seems to be that he's the most narcissistic of the narcissists who find endless fascination in turning the camera on themselves."

It's true that Ross McElwee is extremely charming, but it's not true that Alan Berliner is boring. Alan Berliner is one of the most exciting documentary film-makers working today. His films are among the least boring films I have ever seen in my life, and I can't imagine any other documentarian who takes more care than Alan Berliner to make his films as pleasurable as possible to watch.

But what's objectionable isn't Mr. Moore's experience of Alan Berliner's films as boring (everyone is entitled to their subjective experience). What's objectionable is the way he says it as if it were a fact. Because the frightening truth of the matter is that Mr. Moore does see it as a fact. And it is this confusion of perception with fact that is the most insidious legacy of Mr. Moore's reactionary subliminal messages.

Because this is what I've discovered: most film critics actually don't understand the very first premise of aesthetic theory: namely that there is no truth in aesthetics. Instead, there are truths, stories and/or metaphors that resonate more or less well with one's lived experience.

Some would argue that it's too cumbersome to have to put in "I think" or "in my opinion" every time one ventures an opinion. Fair enough. But there's a different tone that writing takes when its writer is aware of the radical subjectivity of aesthetic appreciation, and this is not it. In fact, most of the film critics I've encountered seem to make that same mistake. They all think they know.

It is this that I find most pernicious in the state of American film criticism: the belief that most film critics seem to have in an objective truth. Their writing belies a simplistic and solipsistic world view which, in my opinion, is one of the things contributing to the widespread suffering that we see in the world. This, I would argue, is also the problem with our president, and with American society generally. We are a nation of egos. In the U.S., the ego is king. And the ego's motto is: "I'm right and you're wrong." Again, we hear the echo of this ideology in Bush's "You're either for us or against us." That facile dualism is at the heart of warfare in general, and the true anti-war films are not films like *Platoon*. They are the films that question dualism and skillfully wrestle it to the ground.

But I digress:

"*I Am a Sex Addict*, an absurd on-camera narrated recounting of his obscenely selfish nature when it comes to women and sex, comes off as an attempt to mock his self-indulgence."

"Obscenely selfish" is an interesting choice of words. Again, we have the ideological underpinnings of Republican-style social conservatism. Some things are "clean," and others "obscene." And again, there is no attempt to question the meaning of that word, or the dualism that it implies. And along with the social conservatism, there is also a concomitant self-righteous moralism. One senses a hint of moral outrage. How dare he treat those women so selfishly? But whence this moral outrage? What's behind it?

Again, we come back to the same duality of good and evil. This particular duality is at the heart of every duality. If we could free ourselves from its tyranny, we would free ourselves from all tyrannies. *Mr. Zahedi is a selfish man, and that's bad*. What we have here is an ideology of politically correct selflessness coupled with a moral injunction. But my film is precisely a refutation of that duality and injunction.

But let us return to the essay:

"Then you realize that he raised money, hired a succession of lovely actresses to simulate (we hope) sex with him, and flew to Europe to re-create trips to film festivals (with earlier films) where he spent a lot of his off-time procuring prostitutes, and trying to convince his various girlfriends that this was "honest" and perfectly "normal.""

First of all, the reviewer here is factually inaccurate, and obviously didn't watch the film very carefully or he would have known that the European film festival scenes were all filmed in San Francisco (which the film clearly states). This kind of inaccuracy in simply reporting the facts is incredibly frustrating for a filmmaker. Shouldn't there be some kind of accountability or fact-checking? These people often end up publishing out-and-out lies, not intentionally but out of laziness, and there's nothing that a filmmaker can do to rectify it, other than to respond in print.

But let me jump ahead to later in the review:

"The film is framed in his address to the camera on his wedding day (Shockingly, he has been married a couple of times.) and flimsily built around his various 'strategies' for coping with his 'addiction,' which he scribbles on a chalkboard."

The irony here is that it is Mr. Moore's punctuation which is flimsy. He inserts a period inside the parenthesis and then begins the next word with a small letter "a." So maybe that was a typo. But his argument is flimsy as well. The construction of my film took over five years. Mr. Moore may not like it, but it's certainly not flimsy. To call it that is either lazy, dishonest, or just plain ignorant.

Let me jump ahead again:

"It takes guts to encourage people, in autobiography, to laugh at you and not with you. There's also the danger that your audience will tune you out as they get to know the real, obnoxious, boring you."

Mr. Moore's assumption that the "real" person (again, that same unquestioning duality) could be ontologically "obnoxious" and "boring" is another instance of the enemy-creating mentality of Mr. Bush and associates. And we also see here another peculiarly American tyranny—the tyranny of the not-boring. Americans are the most frightened people in the world. They are frightened even of themselves, and the thought of spending time with oneself provokes a kind of mental hysteria and its accompanying fascism: the demand to entertain at all times.

But nothing is inherently boring. There are only bored people. People are bored because they have lost the ability to see what is in front of their eyes with freshness and clarity. I would argue that most Hollywood cinema, rather than relieving boredom, only exacerbates it. These films hook us into a wavelength which only reinforces our already reified ways of seeing and thinking, and in the hollowness which this engenders inside us, then encourages a kind of addiction. And it works! Like any addict, we constantly need to up the dose.

But let me jump ahead to the final sentence of the review:

"He's not as fascinating, or as amusing, as he thinks."

Again, we hear the daily call to be amusing. But what's amusing? One man's amusement is another man's paint drying. Many people have found my film amusing. The fact that Mr. Moore does not is neither unimportant nor irrelevant, but it is not the objective truth about my film, as Mr. Moore believes it is. This is the ideology of someone who has never read or understood Nietzsche, never grappled with the ideas of Plato, never gone beyond a Sunday School world view. And this, in my experience, is the state of American film criticism today.

Film Comment, 2006

6
SLINGS AND ARROWS

"A critic is someone who comes onto the battle field after the battle is over and shoots the wounded." —Anonymous

January 27, 2005
My film *I Am a Sex Addict* premieres at the Rotterdam International Film Festival. The very first screening is a press-only screening. About two dozen people are there. The only critic I recognize is Jonathan Rosenbaum. Alexander Payne is there as well (he's an old friend from film school), and most of the attention seems to be directed at him.

I stand at the back to make sure the projection is okay. I wasn't planning to stay, but I can't tear myself away and remain standing the entire movie. My heart soars every time I hear a laugh, and plummets every time an intended laugh is met with silence. Still, the audience sounds like they're enjoying the film, and I am excited and hopeful.

After the screening, I stand near the exit, trying to be approachable without being invasive. The various critics walk past me without saying a word. I can't help wondering if that's just film-critic protocol or if they actually liked it less than I thought.

February 2, 2005

The first review appears in *Screen International*. It is written by Jonathan Romney, who describes the film as "a witty and painful first-person essay with controversial potential" that "artfully treads a line between flippancy and soul-baring seriousness." He also calls it "provocative and courageous."

He also writes that "the film is likely to do well" (!) and that "its arty, bohemian edge should make this a favorite with upmarket indie distributors." He goes on to compare its box-office potential with that of *Tarnation* and *American Splendor*. The review is intelligent, well-written, and overwhelmingly positive. I feel relieved and optimistic about the film's chances for success.

February 17, 2005

The film's second review appears in *Variety*. This one is written by Deborah Young and is less unambiguously positive. Her review begins: "Turning personal obsession into deadpan comedy may seem like a description of Woody Allen's work, but Caveh Zahedi, the actor-director-subject of *I Am a Sex Addict*, creates his own sub-genre of screen narcissism."

"Screen narcissism" doesn't sound very flattering, and I am immediately annoyed. I have been accused of narcissism ad nauseam, and I find the accusation exasperating. I would argue that my films are the exact opposite of narcissism, since I never try to make myself look good and, if anything, exaggerate my character defects. To call my films narcissistic is to equate narcissism with autobiography, which is patently absurd. Were St. Augustine's *Confessions* an instance of narcissism?

April 22, 2005

The film premieres in the U.S. at the Tribeca Film Festival. My sales agent, Cinetic Media, expressly forbids the festival from making video screeners available to the press so as to ensure that no copies are leaked to buyers and that the film is seen only in optimal conditions. *New York Times* critic Stephen Holden, however, is unable to attend the press screening due to a case of shingles, and so someone at the festival surreptitiously slips him a tape (which turns out to be an unfinished rough cut!). Because of the pain he is in from the shingles, Holden is only able to watch part of it, but nevertheless singles it out for special mention in an article about the festival. Here is how he describes me in the *Times*: "Mr. Zahedi, an unattractive creature who resembles a human bug, counters his own creepy narcissism with a deadpan sense of humor that wins you over."

I was mortified. "An unattractive creature who resembles a human bug"? I read this just minutes before having to appear at the theater for a Q&A, and I wanted to crawl into a bug hole and die. Does this even qualify as journalism? Can you just say that about somebody? Aren't there journalistic rules and standards? Isn't that what ombudsmen are for?

I was tempted to write an angry letter to the editor, arguing that Holden's comment was irrelevant, inappropriate, and arguably racist, but my wife dissuaded me, insisting that the less attention drawn to it the better. Still, almost everyone I know has now read that description of me, and I find it deeply humiliating.

On the brighter side, I now have a deeper appreciation for how Gregor Samsa must have felt.

November 30, 2005

My film has been nominated for a Gotham Award for "Best Picture Not Playing at a Theater Near You." What this means is that no distributors have picked up the film. The nominees have been chosen by *Filmmaker* magazine, from a list suggested by festival programmers (who were asked to recommend two films that had not received theatrical distribution). The other nominees are: *Al Otro Lado* (Gustavo Loza), *In a Nutshell* (Don Bernier), *Police Beat* (Robinson Devore), and *Sir! No Sir!* (David Zeiger).

As actress Maria Bello is about to announce the winner, I am suddenly so overtaken with stage fright that I actually pray to God to please not let it be me. I am terrified at the prospect of having to get up in front of all those people and make a televised speech. When she announces my name, I feel like I have just been found guilty and sentenced to death. I make my way to the podium like a man on his way to the gallows. I am so nervous that I can barely speak. But I somehow manage to make people laugh (including Bill Murray!), and I can tell from the applause that I did okay. Now I am ecstatic, and I proceed to have about as much fun that night as I've ever had in my life.

December 15, 2005

Cinetic Media informs me that IFC Films is interested in distributing the film. Jonathan Sehring, the head of IFC, was at the Gotham Awards and liked my acceptance speech. He had apparently never seen the film and asked to watch it. He liked the film and showed it to his boss, who also liked it. The person at IFC who had previously passed on the film had since left the company. And Ryan Werner, who had loved the film when he was at Wellspring but was unable to acquire it because the head of Wellspring hadn't liked it, had since joined IFC. So suddenly, there was a groundswell of support for the film at IFC Films, and all because of the Gotham Award.

April 5, 2006

The film opens theatrically in San Francisco. Mick La Salle, the film critic for the *San Francisco Chronicle*, writes a glowing review. I am thrilled, touched, and impressed by his intelligence, insight, and prose style. His writing is clear, simple, and illuminating. His review begins: "Going in, a few things need to be said about *I Am a Sex Addict*. There's no other film like it. It's embarrassingly frank and self-revealing, sometimes funny, sometimes creepy, sometimes both. It makes sex addiction look almost fun, at first, then ugly and dispiriting. And it just might be the truest film about addiction, of any kind, that has ever been made."

La Salle also writes something about one of the actresses that strikes me as uncanny in its elucidative insight: "[Amanda] Henderson stands out in particular, infusing Devin with a personal philosophy and the sense of some underlying, rueful history." I had never thought about it that way, but he's absolutely right. It's an enlivening experience to discover things about your own film from reading a review.

April 12, 2006

The film opens theatrically in New York. Everyone tells me that the most important review is *The New York Times*, and it is with apprehension that I read it when it appears. My first reaction is "why is it so small?" In the old days, whenever any film would open in New York for at least one week, the *Times* would give it a full review. But now, with so many films coming out each week (almost a dozen other films opened the same day as mine), the *Times* decides in advance which films get full reviews and which films get small reviews. Mine, for some reason, gets a small review.

The review, written by Nathan Lee, is mostly positive, "Mr. Zahedi is charming and disarming even at his most debased," and impeccably well written, "[The film] never mugs for our good will, only our witness, which it rewards with honesty and wit." But I am nevertheless angered by two passages. The first, "The film is a minor triumph of sincerity," strikes me as a back-handed compliment. The second—"But tonic honesty and lack of cool are precisely what saves *Sex Addict* from going too far down the path of *Tarnation*, another exercise in mixed-up aesthetics, sordid subject matter and maniacal self-exposure"—sounds like a dig masquerading as a plaudit. "Mixed-up aesthetics" sounds like I don't know what I'm doing, "sordid subject matter" sounds like my film is exploitative and arguably vulgar, and "maniacal self-exposure" sounds like I'm insane.

IFC Films had recently asked me to start a blog to help promote the film, so I write a rather angry response to Lee's piece, titled "Contra Nathan Lee," which ends with the following paragraph: "None of this would matter very much, and the dig in question could be easily laughed off, if it weren't for the fact that a *New York Times* reviewer has the power to make or break a film, and that an off-handed remark like that can mean the difference between success or failure at the box office. And it's not just the fate of the film that is at stake: it's also the fate of the filmmaker and of his or her ability to make more films in the future. With such power comes a dizzying responsibility, and it saddens me to see film critics wield their formidable power with such breezy insouciance."

Within hours, Lee has posted a thoughtful and detailed rebuttal on my blog. It begins: "I'm not often in the habit of responding to criticism of my criticism, but given the nature of this particular film (confess!), my respect for Mr. Zahedi's work, and certain misconceptions my words have fostered, I thought I'd weigh in. Plus, I'm bored at my day job, and this is way more interesting."

I am so touched by his respectful tone and willingness to respond, that I write an overstated and almost sycophantic apology, which ends with the following: "Thank you again, and I will try harder (with my next film) to earn from you the epithet 'major' in describing my work." Lee soon posts another comment on my blog, writing: "Thanks for the thanks. But wait a second, what is this, a circle jerk?" A bit ashamed at my sudden about-face, I retreat into superciliousness (and pretension): "My contention is that you do not in fact really and truly understand my film because despite your perspicaciousness, you are still seeing it through the looking glass of a previous paradigm, and the film represents something paradigmatically new in the cinematic landscape, something for which there are not yet any viable categories."

Lee realizes, at this point, that the less said the better, and he refrains from responding to my last comment.

April 13, 2006

In a review for the right wing *New York Post,* film critic V. A. Musetto writes: "How many times can you listen to this obnoxious man's neurotic ramblings? And, you must wonder, what in hell did all those beautiful, intelligent women ever see in this scrawny, neurotic, sicko nerd?" My publicist is mortified by the viciousness of the attack, but to my way of thinking, Musetto's remarks are so over-the-top as to be almost comical. Consequently, I am less upset by his review than I was by the infinitely more positive but also more incisive review by Lee.

Nevertheless, I decide once again to respond on my blog, with an entry entitled: "V.A. Musetto Is a Sex Addict." My admittedly tenuous argument is that the vituperativeness of Musetto's attack seems to belie some sexual addiction of his own, and that his self-righteousness and need to distance himself from me and my behavior is evidence of my film hitting a little too close to home. I have noticed that it's often those who feel most conflicted about their own sexual desires who express the most indignation about my own.

April 25, 2006

The good news is that Anthony Lane has decided to do a full review of *I Am A Sex Addict* for *The New Yorker*, arguably the most prestigious magazine in America. The bad news is that the review he writes is trivial and inane, more of a pretext for him to make sex jokes than a serious discussion of the film. For instance, he writes, "Prostitutes, my ass: with this grade of self-attention, I think we know what this guy's favorite turn-on has to be." The imputation of narcissism rubs me the wrong way. Plus, he doesn't seem even to begin to grasp the radicalness of the film, writing that "the overriding reason to see the film" is my resemblance to Harpo Marx. Whatever my resemblance to Harpo Marx might be, it's hardly the overriding reason to see this movie.

I write an angry response on my blog, despite the fact that everyone I know tells me I shouldn't cross Lane, because he is so "powerful." But I feel that it is ridiculous that he be allowed to write such inanities. What has film reviewing come to? Is it just another form of entertainment? Lane's reviews remind me of those caricaturists who used to appear on *Bozo the Clown* and who could take any written word and within seconds transform it into a visual image (of, say, a tree or a house). His reviews are entirely about him and his formidable wit, and not about the films they purport to describe. Talk about narcissism!

On my blog, I write: "The breezy, ironic tone of most film critics (of whom Mr. Lane is only one of many, unfortunately), while arguably entertaining, in the end serves no one, but only contributes to the ongoing debasement of public discourse." The blog posting ends sarcastically with: "You're very funny, Mr. Lane. Keep up the great work." Needless to say, he doesn't respond to my posting. But what he does do is rewrite the review for the following week's briefs.

New Yorker critic Richard Brody had already written a favorable (and insightful) capsule review of the film that had appeared the week before Lane's much longer review had come out. The week after my posting, Brody's capsule was rewritten by Lane and became markedly harsher and more negative. Lane's initial review began: "There is one overriding reason to see *I Am a Sex Addict* and it has nothing do with sex." The revised capsule review begins: "Dedicated smut hunters will want to stay away from this film, for the good reason that it offers a minimum—and not always a bare minimum—of actual sex." The two sentences say the same thing, but the first sounds like a recommendation, and the second like a warning.

April 29, 2006

The film opens in L.A. on my birthday. The *Los Angeles Times* film critic, Carina Chocano, writes an irate review, the title of which is "Narcissist Turns Camera on Himself." She writes: "It probably goes against current trends in addiction treatment to suggest that shame was appropriate, not a demon to be exorcised at the expense of his partners' mental well-being." Her review smacks of a wounded feminist consciousness projecting past personal resentments onto my character. This has been a fairly predictable response, although by no means has it been the only response.

The problem with such a review is that it is almost entirely given over to a knee-jerk moralistic castigation of my character, without any understanding of the complex dialectic between my character as it is portrayed in the film and me, the filmmaker who is portraying that character in a critical light. Granted, it complicates matters that the filmmaker is playing himself at a younger age, but this confusion and moral ambiguity is precisely what makes the film complex and interesting.

Unfortunately, Chocano's review seems to have a big effect on the box office, because the film tanks in L.A. In other cities, there were both positive and negative reviews, but in L.A., the only other review was a wishy-washy take in the *L.A. Weekly*, so nondescript as to be the equivalent of having no review at all.

June 26, 2006

I Am a Sex Addict is nearing the end of its theatrical run. As the film makes its way from the urban centers to the more out-of-the-way places, the reviews have tended to get more negative, more indignant, less well written, and less insightful. In the *Orlando Sentinel*, Roger Moore writes: "Zahedi, a Woody-Allen homely little weasel with a thing for drugs (his *I Was Possessed by God* recounts a vivid mushroom trip), women, and most of all, himself, creates these little pseudo-biographical essays that suggest he's either a spoiled jerk with access to cameras, or a wit whose jerkiness is something of a pose." In the *Salt Lake Tribune*, Sean Means writes: "Making this confessional film may have been therapeutic for Zahedi, but it's pure torture for an audience to watch him replay his sexual history as he narrates his constant rationalizations." And in the *Tucson Weekly Review*, James DiGiovanna writes: "He may be the most self-involved person on the face of the Earth, and he plays himself in this unbelievably uncomprehending self-examination."

Still, the majority of reviews have been positive, many of them overwhelmingly so. The Rotten Tomatoes website's "tomatometer" lists 17 positive reviews as opposed to 11 negative ones, for an average rating of 6.2 out of 10, which is actually quite good. That means it got better reviews than *X-Men: The Last Stand*, *The Da Vinci Code*, *Ice Age: The Meltdown*, *Pirates of the Caribbean: Dead Man's Chest*, *Nacho Libre*, and *The Omen*, all of which made fortunes at the box office.

Also, I've gotten so used to the negative reviews that they no longer make my blood boil the way they used to, and I no longer feel the same need to blog about them. I've been surprised by the hostility, the smugness, and the mind-boggling ignorance of an alarming number of film reviewers, but I've also learned not to expect much. It's unfortunate that there aren't more film-literate reviewers out there who not only write well but are also able to shed light on a film and provide a way of thinking about it that stimulates the imagination rather than shutting it down.

It seems to me that even a review of a bad film should be able to help one see it in a more interesting way and to enliven one's thinking about it. A good example is the negative but brilliant review by film critic Manny Farber of Martin Scorsese's *Taxi Driver*, entitled "The Power & the Gory." Farber is ruthless in his critique of the film, but the review somehow adds to the experience of watching the movie rather than diminishing it.

Most of the negative reviews of my film, on the other hand, were simply a motley assortment of pre-existing prejudices and opinions masquerading as ideas. What I have found most disturbing in all this is the smugness with which people who know very little about film history, and who, in some cases, were reassigned to the film section of their newspaper after having covered sports or restaurants for a number of years, feel qualified to pass judgment on films they simply don't have the critical background to understand.

I found only one critic who had the humility to at least acknowledge his lack of knowledge about film (although he gave me a negative review anyway). Jeremy Buckley, in the *Daily Nebraskan* wrote: "Maybe it's because I don't personally have any experience with being addicted to sex, or my lack of background in art films, but it seems this film is meant for a crowd of people that aren't looking for a specific issue to be resolved in a movie." Now that's honest at least, and surprisingly open-minded.

If more critics were humble enough to be able to at least imagine that there might be other ways of thinking about a particular film beside their own, the whole cultural conversation about cinema would immediately take on a much more inspiring (and respectful) tone. There would be fewer low blows and a sincere interest in trying to understand a film's radical otherness. The best critics, like Manny Farber or André Bazin, invariably deepen our relationship not only to cinema but also to the world in which we all must learn to live.

Film Comment, 2006

7
THE *VERTIGO* TOUR

Last April, I was having coffee with *Filmmaker* magazine editor Scott Macaulay in New York and he asked me if I would be interested in writing a piece on San Francisco in the movies for *Film in Focus*. I'm usually strapped for cash, so I said yes. But when I asked him to be more specific, he said I could write about pretty much anything I wanted. Anything? I thought about it for a second, and then mentioned to him that there was a *Vertigo* tour in San Francisco and perhaps I could write about that. He thought that was a great idea (really?) and I agreed to write the piece once I was back in San Francisco (I was living in Rome at the time, but that's another story).

This October, soon after returning to San Francisco, I got an email from Scott asking if I was still interested in writing about the *Vertigo* tour. I was still strapped for cash, so I said yes. I looked online to find out more about the tour and I was stunned to learn that it costs $285 for the five-hour tour, and $585 for the ten-hour tour. Ten hours?

I emailed Scott and explained the situation—namely, that I couldn't actually afford to take the tour, and would he be able to pick up the tab? He struck a deal with the tour guide, Jesse Warr, and asked if I would prefer the five-hour tour or the ten-hour tour. I expressed my strong preference for the five-hour tour, as well as my inability to imagine doing any one thing for ten hours.

Later that week, I was playing racquetball with my friend Sam Green, the director of the Oscar-nominated documentary *The Weather Underground*, and I mentioned that I was going to take the *Vertigo* tour. "Can I come?" Sam asked. "Gee," I said. "I don't know. It's kind of pricey. I can ask Scott if he can pay for you to come along too, but I kind of doubt it." "Maybe I could take pictures," said Sam. "That's a great idea," I said, "because I don't really know how to use my digital camera."

When I got home from racquetball, there was an email from Scott asking if I could also take pictures during the *Vertigo* tour. What a perfect opportunity to ask about Sam. I played the Oscar nomination angle, and Scott said okay.

I told Sam it was a go, and the first thing he said was, "Great. But just so you know, I'm not a great photographer. I'm okay, but I'm nothing special." "No problem," I said, "you can't be worse than me."

Jesse Warr picked me up at my apartment at 1:30pm on a Sunday. I brought a DVD of the film as well as my computer so that I could freeze-frame certain stills and take pictures at those locations. Sam was supposed to meet us there, but he was running late, so we decided to meet him at Mission Dolores, the California Mission where James Stewart follows Kim Novak into the cemetery.

During the car ride there, Jesse Warr started in on his tour guide spiel, and I immediately wanted to jump out of the car. I am deeply allergic to lectures of any kind, and even the slightest trace of pontification makes me start to hyperventilate. I kept interrupting him and changing the subject so that I could breathe, but he was the kind of tour guide who continues to plow through with whatever he happens to be saying, whether you are still alive to hear it or not.

I was relieved to see Sam waiting for us in front of the Mission. As we passed a diorama purporting to depict life in the early Mission days, Jesse started to tell us the history of the California Indians who once inhabited this region. Quick, Sam, take some photos before I blow my brains out.

Sam started taking pictures, but we quickly realized that it was impossible to replicate Hitchcock's images exactly using Sam's digital camera because Hitchcock had access to a much wider variety of lenses than Sam. Also, Hitchcock had access to movie lights.

I did my best to try to imitate the body language of Jimmy Stewart, but I was dressed wrong, and I had no hat. Also, he's taller than me. Also, he's a better actor.

The cemetery has changed considerably since Hitchcock shot the film in 1957, but how is it possible that the gravestones would have been moved? Had he added fake gravestones? Nothing seemed to match.

Our next stop was Madeleine's apartment building. It looked remarkably unchanged, but it was still almost impossible to figure out where exactly the actors and the camera had stood. At this point, we were starting to get a little discouraged. Sam was right about not being a great photographer, and it was becoming increasingly clear that our "before" and "after" pictures would suck.

Jesse took us to Scottie's apartment, and there it was, exactly like in the film, except that the red door had been painted white, the railing had been replaced, and a large hedge had been planted in front which obscured the view. Still, Jesse and I did our best to imitate the exact body language of Kim Novak and James Stewart, and it was around now that we finally started to bond.

Jesse seemed to enjoy the idea of imitating Kim Novak and said that had he known we would do this, he would have dressed for the part. It was then that the irony of the situation struck me: here we were, two strangers trying our best to recapture a moment from the past and act the part of someone else, which is precisely what *Vertigo* is about. In that sense, the *Vertigo* tour perfectly mimics the central conceit of the movie, and allows fans of the film to inhabit the implicit contradiction of the film, the always impossible but all-too-human attempt to make our illusions real.

Filmmaker Magazine, 2008

8
SHUTTING ROBERT BRESSON'S GATE

I once met Robert Bresson. This was in 1984. I had recently moved to Paris and had just seen *L'Argent* in an almost empty theater (there was only one other person in the room). Seeing it was one of those mind-blowing experiences, and I immediately decided that it was the greatest film ever made. I was staying with a friend at the time who, hearing me gush on and on, told me she had Bresson's phone number and that I should call him and tell him myself. I phoned immediately, and he answered the phone. I explained to him that I was an American filmmaker visiting Paris and, after gushing about his film, asked if I could meet him. For some reason he said yes, and invited me to come visit him the next day at his apartment.

His apartment was surprisingly modest, its walls crammed from floor to ceiling with books. A pretty, youngish woman who I assumed to be his wife darted in and out throughout our conversation. When I asked him what other filmmakers he liked, he replied that he hated all of contemporary cinema. I was taken aback. He hated everyone? He said yes, but also added that he hadn't seen a film in twenty years. I found this hard to believe. He then admitted that he had in fact seen two films in the last twenty years, films that he had been dragged to by his friends who insisted that he had to see the work of this particular director. "Which director?" I asked. He couldn't remember the director's name, but he described (with great aversion) both films to me. "You mean *Rear Window*?" I said. "*Rear Window* by Hitchcock? And *Rope*?" "That's his name, Hitchcock!" Bresson exclaimed. I was stunned. "You didn't like *Rear Window*?" I asked. "I hated it," he replied. "Everything in it was fake. Nothing was real." "But it's an allegory," I retorted. "Exactly!" he answered triumphantly. "It's an allegory. I hate allegories."

I was thrown by this comment, being myself at the time a lover of allegories. So I changed the topic, and asked him what he was working on. He told me he was writing a new book on film, a kind of sequel to his first book (this sequel has yet to see the light of day). He also told me how hurt he was by the insinuations of certain film critics that the only reason he had cast the Minister of Culture's daughter in *L'Argent* was in order to obtain financing from the Ministry of Culture. I, of course, had no idea that he had even cast the Minister of Culture's daughter in the film, let alone that there had been any controversy. He insisted that he had cast the Minister of Culture's daughter because she had been the best person for the part, and that it had absolutely nothing to do with her being the daughter of the Minister of Culture. It saddened me to hear Bresson defending himself to me, a neophyte filmmaker with no reason to question his sincerity.

When I left his apartment, he asked me to be sure to shut the gate on my way out. I assured him that I would. As I walked down the stairs, he called out to make sure not to forget to shut the gate. I assured him I would remember. As I reached the gate and opened it, he called out to me again to make sure the gate was shut before leaving. I reassured him one last time, then walked through the gate and shut it behind me with a heavy heart.

9
ADDERALL DIARY

December 10, 2013
I receive an email informing us that our project (about the artist Joseph Cornell's relationship with a waitress in the early sixties) has been accepted to Cinemart.

January 21, 2014
We receive our list of meeting requests. We have 37 meetings scheduled over a three-day period. The last time I was at Cinemart (in 1994), I only had three meeting requests.

January 25, 2014
7am. Jan, my astrophysicist friend who recently discovered the age of the universe to be 13.8 billion years (give or take 138 million), picks us up from the airport and drives us to Rotterdam.

8am. The hotel receptionist informs us that we can't check in until 3pm. Bummer. I had been looking forward to catching up on some sleep. Jan offers to let us sleep at his house in Amsterdam so we drive all the way back to Amsterdam and go to bed.

2pm. Jan drives us back to Rotterdam.

4pm. We check in at Cinemart headquarters where we run into Gabe Klinger who tells me that Jim Jarmusch is executive producing his next film. I feel a surge of envy.

6pm. My friend David, who lives in Amsterdam, brings us a week's supply of weed, but the hotel receptionist informs us that we can't smoke pot in our hotel room because it's a non-smoking room and all the smoking rooms are taken.

David asks her where the nearest coffee shop is.

"Dutch coffee shop or regular coffee shop?" she asks.

"Dutch coffee shop."

We enter a "Dutch coffee shop" and are greeted by a variety of cannabis for sale. I ask the server to describe the different highs. She tells me that the more expensive the weed, the higher you get.

We purchase the most expensive kind and get very, very high.

January 26, 2014

10am. The Cinemart staff introduce themselves and do a PowerPoint presentation on what to expect.

11:30am. Two Cinemart staffers sit down with us to go over our meetings list and give us background information on the various companies that have requested meetings.

1pm. Arnold and I spend the afternoon reading through the industry manual. We contact another dozen or so people to set up additional meetings.

5pm. We get stoned and work on the script.

10pm. We go see the new Jim Jarmusch film.

January 27, 2014

9:30am. The first sales agent we meet with likes the idea of casting John Hawkes as Joseph Cornell but is less keen on Jeremy Irons.

10:30am. The second sales agent we meet with likes the idea of casting Jeremy Irons as Joseph Cornell but is less keen on John Hawkes.

11am. The person from the West Sweden film fund explains to us that if we do our post-production in West

Sweden, we can get the regional film fund to cover all of our post-production costs. And if we hire any West Swedish cast or crew, the West Sweden film fund will pay their salaries as well. West Sweden, here we come.

11:30am. A French distributor tells us she gives advances on films when she loves the script. She seems very taken by the story of Joseph Cornell but dislikes our title, *The Sky Is Blue Like an Orange.*

12pm. The producer from Rohfilm explains that if we shoot our interiors in Germany, we become eligible for German regional film fund subsidies. West Sweden? Germany? How to decide?

12:30pm. I love the British Film Institute representative because, unlike most of the people we've been speaking to, she seems to get my jokes. Unfortunately, we don't qualify for BFI money because: 1) I'm not British, 2) my writing partner is not British, 3) Cornell was not British, 4) Jeremy Irons is British but one British actor isn't enough to qualify, 5) Carey Mulligan is British but two British actors aren't enough to qualify, and 6) Cornell was a Francophile. We decide to make our next film a biopic of William Shakespeare.

2–4pm. Jet lag is starting to set in and I'm having a hard time staying awake. As a result, the afternoon meetings are a blur. I can't remember much except that we should consider shooting all of our interiors in Belgium.

Arnold tells me that my low energy isn't making the best impression on would-be investors and he gives me some Ritalin. I've never done Ritalin before but am happy to try it. It wakes me up and makes me uncharacteristically chatty and gregarious.

4:30pm. A British sales agent explains to us that having our project invited to Cinemart is the kiss of death because they tend to pick uncommercial projects.

5pm. We request a meeting with the representative from agnès b.'s production company with the assumption that agnès b. finances the films she likes (Harmony Korine, Gaspar Noé, etc.) out of pocket. The representative from agnès b. explains to us that they apply for government money just like everyone else and that when people ask for meetings with them because they think agnès b. has private money to spend, it's a real turn-off. Oops.

5:30pm. We meet with a British producer based in Cologne. I love this guy. Unlike most of the people we've met with, he's willing to try to find private financing and thinks outside the box. I shake his hand and tell him it's a deal. Cologne, here we come.

6pm. Still high on Ritalin, I start walking up to random people at the cocktail party and making small talk. This is very unlike me but it feels great. I've never been this friendly in my entire life.

7:30pm. I befriend a bunch of Israeli filmmakers, including the guy who directed *The Band's Visit*, a film I loved. I also meet an Israeli producer who agrees to partner up on my supernatural thriller set in Jerusalem. Ritalin is fantastic!

10:30pm. The thing about Ritalin is that when you come down, you come down hard.

January 28, 2014

9:30am. We meet with a producer from Pandora, the German production company that produced the new Jarmusch film. I like him right away. He has deep, sad, world-weary eyes and a gravitas that is rare in the States. He tells us that if we shoot in Berlin, he can probably raise about $500,000 total, but that we need to have the rest of the budget already in place.

10am. We meet with another producer from Cologne, which apparently has the largest regional film fund, even bigger than Berlin's. Back to Cologne.

11:30am. We meet with Antoine Simkin, a French producer who did the special effects for *Delicatessen*, *City of Lost Children*, and *Amélie*. He raves about *I Am A Sex Addict* and I take an instant liking to him. He looks a lot like Godard so I pitch my Godard/Anna Karina film project. He seems interested and offers to look into the rights issues involved. I've got a good feeling about this guy.

12:30pm We meet with a sad-eyed French producer. I keep thinking "He looks so sad." I like people with sad eyes but I can't help wondering what he's so sad about and find it hard to concentrate on what he's saying.

2–3pm. I'm falling asleep from jet lag. I ask Arnold for more Ritalin.

3:30pm. We meet with someone from Kickstarter. I explain to her why I think Kickstarter is the latest manifestation of capitalism's encroachment into every aspect of life–even friendship–and how Kickstarter has pushed the commodification of friendship to a new low. She does a masterful job reframing Kickstarter as the antidote to capitalism–as a way for people to join together and support each other without reliance on market forces. She completely changes my way of thinking about it. Kickstarter, here we come.

4pm. We meet with Keith Griffiths, the legendary British producer of the Brothers Quay films. He has occupied a place in my imagination for over twenty years, so I am thrilled to finally be meeting him. I do my very best to charm him into coming on board as a co-producer but he seems charm-proof. At one point, I ask him, "Are you not finding me incredibly charming?" He says: "You're very charming, but I'm not charmed."

5pm. Cinemart offers two cash prizes (30,000 Euros for best co-production and 5,000 Euros for best project), so every project has to pitch to the jurors. It is the end of the day so I can't tell how much of it is exhaustion and how much of it is directed specifically towards me, but rarely have I encountered more unfriendly interlocutors. They just stare blankly with their arms folded and studiously refuse to laugh at any of my jokes. I'm noticeably less charming when I feel unloved and my pitch quickly devolves into incoherence. Arnold tries to step in to do damage control but I interrupt him to try to engage them in a meta-discussion about how we're flailing here in the face of their seeming hostility. They insist they are just being neutral but I beg to differ. Their hostility deepens. Finally, they declare "Thank you very much" which means "Goodbye, we've had enough of you."

5:30pm. We meet with the representative from Soda, a British arthouse producer and distributor. She laughs at all my jokes and I love her right away.

6:00pm. We get stoned and work on the script.

January 29, 2014
9:30am. We meet with a Danish producer who explains to us that if we cast a Danish actor in the lead, we might be eligible to qualify for Danish Film Fund money. I mention to him that Mads Mikkelson had been on our list to play Cornell. He informs us that Viggo Mortensen is also Danish. Viggo was the first person we had thought of for the role but his agent had told us he wasn't reading any scripts that weren't already financed so we had moved on. Suddenly, he's back on our list.

10:30am. We meet with Koyo Yamashita, a Japanese theater owner and art film distributor. He is a fan of *I Am A Sex Addict* and asks me to send him a link to *The Sheik and I* as well as to the box set materials that Factory 25 is releasing sometime this century. I like this guy.

12pm. We meet with a potential co-producer from New Zealand who talks us into shooting the interiors in New Zealand.

3:30pm. We meet with a potential co-producer from Nottingham and crack Robin Hood jokes. I like this guy. Nottingham it is.

4:30pm. We meet with an American representative from a sales agency that had rejected *The Sheik and I* so I arrive at the meeting still holding a grudge. He does an excellent job persuading me to let it go. This guy is straight-talking and to the point. He tells us: "John Hawkes is worth nothing" vis a vis foreign sales. I tell him that other sales agents we've spoken to were excited at the idea of having John Hawkes in the film, but he insists that's because they've never tried to sell a film he stars in. Hmm. Could it be that the film he tried to sell had other deficiencies?

5pm. We meet with a delightful Danish producer with whom we hit it off right away. She mentions that she is currently producing a film that stars Viggo Mortensen. Arnold and I look at each other, incredulous. She tells us he's wonderful to work with and asks us to send her the script right away. Danish co-production here we come.

6pm. I'm exhausted from three days of meetings and decide to cancel my multiple dinner plans, get stoned, and work on the script some more so we can send it to the Danes tonight.

9pm. Arnold needs to eat something so we go to the mediocre Chinese restaurant in the lobby of the hotel where we run into the delightful Danish producer and her equally delightful Swedish producing partner. We like them both a lot and they seem to like us too and, for a brief moment, all is well in the world. We return to the hotel, finish the script, and send it off.

January 30, 2014
8am. I hate to throw away our remaining pot stash and contemplate taking it with me back to the States but Arnold talks me out of it. With a heavy heart, I flush it down the toilet at the Amsterdam airport and board the plane.

9
ON LARS VON TRIER'S
NYMPHOMANIAC

Two weeks ago, I received an email asking me if I would be interested in writing about Lars von Trier's *Nymphomaniac*. I hadn't seen the film yet but was dying to. I am a HUGE von Trier fan and had already been wowed by the film's promotional campaign—the suggestive yet subtle parentheses, the orgasm faces, and the cornucopia of trailers. As is often the case with von Trier, I felt simultaneously grateful for and jealous of his brilliance. I myself had made a film called *I am a Sex Addict* and was dreading the inevitability that he would tackle the subject of sex far more brilliantly than I had.

I should explain that when I decided to become a filmmaker, my overriding goal was to become the greatest filmmaker of all time. To me, this was the whole point. It was about ego, not art. I saw it as a kind of contest. The point was to win—to outdo everyone else.

As my understanding of the medium deepened and I began to be awed by the vertiginous accomplishments of my predecessors, the first faint stirrings of humility began to set in. I still saw filmmaking as a contest, but I was no longer taking my victory for granted. I was beginning to see my own limitations.

In *The Anxiety of Influence*, Harold Bloom argues that every artist is always engaged in a struggle to outdo some predecessor. For me, Tarkovsky was always the filmmaker to beat, because his films struck me as the most spiritual. But how anyone could ever outdo him was difficult to imagine.

One night, I went to a screening of *Breaking the Waves*. I had seen previous von Trier films but had never been particularly impressed by them. *Breaking the Waves*, on the other hand, took my breath away.

The lights went off and the film began. This was something I had never experienced before. I felt like I was watching, shot for shot, the film that I myself would have made had I been more brilliant, more accomplished, and more spiritually evolved. It was like having a two-hour orgasm. It was the most ecstatic viewing experience of my life. *Breaking the Waves* became my favorite film of all time. As far as I was concerned, von Trier had just given Tarkovsky a serious run for his money.

I felt the same way about *The Idiots*, von Trier's follow-up film. Shot in accordance with the Dogme 95 "rules of chastity" that von Trier (and Dogme 95 co-founder Thomas Vinterberg) came up with as a "rescue action" to save cinema from the "golden calf" of "predictability," this hand-held film shot with a consumer mini-DV camera was unlike anything I had ever seen. The moral anguish and political despair of that film hit very close to him. It became my new favorite film of all time.

When I heard von Trier's next film was going to be a musical using a hundred mini-DV cameras, I was jealous. My dream had always been to one day make a Busby Berkeley-style musical and, once again, he had beaten me to the punch. My fear was that his musical would be very much like the musical I myself had been envisioning, except much better. When I finally saw *Dancer in the Dark*, I loved the film but felt that the musical sequences didn't live up to the promise of what a hundred cameras could capture. I couldn't help thinking that I could have done a better job with the choreography or, at least, the choreography in my head seemed better to me than the choreography in that film.

The Five Obstructions, on the other hand, was a film I never could have imagined. The premise of the film — hiring his former mentor to remake his short film masterpiece five times with five different obstructions — was such an act of loving kindness towards Jorgen Leth while at the same time being so bold, so off-beat, so mischievous, and so inimitably von Trier. It immediately became my favorite documentary of all time. Von Trier had done it again — with his first documentary, he had both transcended and reinvented the whole genre.

Around this time, I was making my *Tripping with Caveh* series (of which only one episode, featuring singer/songwriter Will Oldham, was ever completed). The person in the world I most wanted to trip with was von Trier so I contacted Jorgen Leth (whom I had met at Sundance when *The Five Obstructions* premiered there) and obtained von Trier's contact info. I wrote him a letter but I couldn't bring myself to send it. I was too intimidated.

When I heard that von Trier's next film, *Dogville*, would be shot on a sound stage and would use chalk outlines to represent locations, I became jealous once again. As a big fan of all things Brechtian, I'd had a very similar idea for a film but von Trier pulled it off at a level that far surpassed anything I had envisioned. I was disappointed, however, by the gratuitous violence of the ending. It reminded me of a little boy who painstakingly builds a huge tower out of popsicle sticks only to knock the whole thing down in one peremptory gesture. There's a certain perverse thrill in doing that, but there's also an empty feeling afterwards.

Manderlay, von Trier's sequel to *Dogville*, was panned by most critics and did poorly at the box office—but I loved it. Never had I seen racism explored so boldly and directly and unapologetically. Screw the wimpy politically correct critics. Von Trier was still the most interesting filmmaker in the world.

When I heard he was making a horror film called *Antichrist*, I was jealous yet again. What a great title for a movie. And what an interesting film. The scene where Willem Dafoe's character discovers that his wife has been deliberately putting their child's left shoe on his right foot, and his right shoe on the left foot, is one of the great reveals in the history of cinema. Von Trier was continuing to push the envelope of the medium, but now Tarkovsky was a more palpable influence. It was becoming clear that Tarkovsky was, for him as well as for me, the filmmaker to beat.

When I finally saw *Melancholia*, the Tarkovsky influence was still noticeable, clearly unexorcised, but Wow! Here was von Trier taking on global warming, nuclear annihilation, and death—all in one film. Von Trier's answer to Tarkovsky's *The Sacrifice*, the ending of *Melancholia* ranks alongside the end of *Andrei Rublev* and *The Devil, Probably* as one of the greatest endings ever. It became my new favorite film of all time.

And then I heard he was making a film called *Nymphomaniac*. If I had been jealous before, I was really jealous now. What a great title. What a great subject. So commercial. So promising. So tantalizing. Several critics had called it von Trier's magnum opus. One wrote that von Trier had recently read all of Proust and that *Nymphomaniac* was his response to *In Search of Lost Time*. I'd been working on my own Proustian opus for years, so I had some resistance to seeing von Trier's latest masterpiece—afraid that I'd be discouraged and demoralized by von Trier's inevitably more brilliant riff on Proust. Being asked to write about it forced me to overcome my resistance.

For those who haven't yet seen it, von Trier's two-part opus is about (you guessed it) a nymphomaniac, Joe (played by Charlotte Gainsbourg, with Stacy Martin as young Joe), who is beaten and left unconscious in an empty alleyway before being discovered by a Good Samaritan, Seligman (Stellan Skarsgård), who takes her to his home to convalesce. The film cuts back and forth between the framing device of the discussion between Joe and Seligman, and the story of Joe's nymphomania.

I wanted to love it. And there were many things about the film I did love: the dialogue, the visuals (indebted, once again, to Tarkovsky), the casting of Martin, and the sheer transgressive rage that was evident throughout. I also loved the scene in which Joe prioritizes her desire to win a childish bet over a man's desire to impregnate his wife who has been having difficulty conceiving, the scene in which a cheated-on wife brings her children to Joe's apartment to guilt-trip their father, and the scene in which Joe gives a repressed pedophile a blow job out of compassion for the tragedy of his condition.

But my overall feeling was one of disappointment. Was this what von Trier wanted to say about human sexuality? Was this what he chose to make a five-hour film about? But I wasn't just disappointed. There was something else going on, something far more unsettling than mere disappointment. In *Nymphomaniac*, von Trier blithely dispenses with any of the psychological acuity and narrative plausibility that his previous films, however Brechtian, always maintained.

I should say here that the version I watched is the truncated four-hour theatrical version, not the original five-hour director's cut. I imagine that the five-hour version is much, much better. There were several episodes in the film that seemed truncated and underdeveloped. As a result, both the psychology and the plausibility suffer. One of the scenes deleted from the four-hour version was, apparently, an extreme close-up of female genitalia, so close as to become abstract. Now that's a great idea for a shot. It's so graphic as to become literally "graphic" and thereby no longer "pornographic." I'm sure there were other amazing things lost in the abridged version.

I've read that von Trier approved of the four-hour version without ever actually watching it and without editing it himself. That's odd. Why would any film-maker go to all the trouble of writing, shooting, and editing a film only to release a version that he has not cut down himself or even bothered to watch? And why release a truncated version at all? Von Trier certainly has the clout to insist on the five-hour version. The film has already been divided into two parts. Adding half an hour to each part wouldn't have made the film significantly less marketable.

The answer, I believe, has to do with von Trier's quest for self-acceptance. Because what's most striking (and most radical) about *Nymphomaniac* isn't the film's relentless cataloguing of sexual and moral transgressions—it's his almost rabid attack on the very notion of "art."

Von Trier had already hinted at his mixed feelings about art in the Dogme 95 manifesto when he (and Vinterberg) wrote the following vow of chastity: "I swear as a director to refrain from personal taste! I am no longer an artist." Perhaps this is the only way to outdo Tarkovsky—by repudiating the aesthetic assumptions with which he operates. Because, frankly, Tarkovsky is unbeatable if one agrees to abide by the rules and protocols of spiritualist cinema—a certain notion of seriousness, narrative and psychological plausibility, and stunning cinematography. It's like trying to outdo Bach while still obeying the rules of harmony. Forget it. The only way is to pull a John Cage maneuver and throw out harmony altogether. *Nymphomaniac* represents von Trier's latest attempt to break the rules of arthouse cinema in order to find another way, a new way, without the arguably tired and oppressive aesthetic constraints under which we all labor. He has made a valiant and even formidable attempt to dislodge Tarkovsky from the Mount Olympus of cinema and to knock down at the same time the whole crumbling edifice of good taste and manners. In *Nymphomaniac*, von Trier is, in a sense, shitting (or pissing or ejaculating) all over Tarkovsky, in an attempt to sully everything he stands for.

I applaud the attempt and I agree with the necessity of such a move. But I think his latest approach misses something crucial. No matter how hard he tries, it will always be a losing proposition. Because the film's true precursor is not Proust (who followed the rules of good prose) but the Marquis de Sade. Von Trier has often exhibited a sadistic streak and this is one of the things he has been criticized for. This sadism is visible in every single one of the films I've mentioned with the exception of *Melancholia*, in which von Trier's compassion for humanity outweighs his rage. And this sadism has been directed not only at his characters but towards his audience as well.

I, personally, love this aspect of von Trier's work and recognize a similar sadism in my own work. Where I part ways with von Trier is in his frontal attack on art. For me, art is of God. And I, personally, no longer feel any need to shit (or piss or ejaculate) on God.

Nymphomaniac resembles the work of de Sade not only in its ostensible subject matter—sexual transgression—but also in its florid 18th-century enlightenment literary style and in the film's framing device of a philosophical conversation about what the social constraints on sexual freedom should or shouldn't be. But de Sade wrote most of his books in order to get off. He was an obsessive masturbator who was trying to turn himself on. Von Trier is also trying to get himself off but his obsession is less sexual than artistic. He is trying to turn himself on artistically and his need for artistic transgression has brought him to the current aesthetic impasse that is *Nymphomaniac.*

In Sex Addicts Anonymous, a sex addict is defined as someone who sexualizes their anger. Different people act out their anger in different ways. Some drink. Some gamble. Some overeat. Von Trier has been acting out his anger in his filmmaking for a long time—which is, I think, healthy and even salubrious. But at a certain point, acting out becomes a way of avoiding authentic transcendence.

The Sex Addicts Anonymous scene in *Nymphomaniac* is particularly telling. The 12-step program is treated with contempt and derision by von Trier who doesn't even bother trying to get the details right or grapple in any real way with the complexity of the issues involved. In short, there is no higher power in *Nymphomaniac.* The notion of a higher power is, in fact, treated as a sham. People are essentially evil and there is no God.

In a recent interview, von Trier, who was raised atheist but converted to Catholicism in the wake of a spiritual experience that immediately preceded *Breaking the Waves,* claimed he no longer believes in God. Is there a correlation between von Trier's recent atheism and the dip in artistic quality that *Nymphomaniac* represents? Another way to put it is that von Trier no longer believes in Art with a capital A. There is a slapdash quality to *Nymphomaniac* at the level of the writing, the casting, and the release of the truncated version that represents something new (and, in my opinion, unfortunate) in his work. He just doesn't seem to give a shit anymore—at least not in the old way.

On the one hand, this is demoralizing. On the other hand, it makes me feel that maybe I still have a chance to outdo him. Perhaps he has thrown in the towel of art as an act of charity to all of the other filmmakers out there who continue to be oppressed by the burdensome ideal of "great art." Perhaps *Nymphomaniac* represents von Trier's Christ moment—his willingness to take on the sins and scorn of the world for the sake of others. And in a way it is. But it's also a sign of a certain exhaustion.

Let's face it: the guy is insanely prolific. He has four children. He struggles with phobias and depression. If you look at recent pictures of him, it's clear that he's not getting enough sleep. He's working too hard, but his ambition is such that he can't help himself. He's driven by something he can't fully control, like the Marquis de Sade.

It's difficult and undoubtedly hubristic to criticize a filmmaker of such brilliance, especially one who has demonstrated such a deep spiritual engagement throughout his career. Perhaps one should always give von Trier the benefit of the doubt. Maybe I just don't get what he's doing anymore. Maybe he's functioning at a level so high above me that I can't even understand the terms in which he is currently operating. But I used to feel so in sync with his work and, with this film, I no longer do. Besides, I have no compass with which to view his work other than my own subjectivity.

There has always been a childishly naughty streak in von Trier's work and personality. This is something to which I can totally relate. Fuck maturity. Fuck what other people think is proper. Fuck all norms. But where does it end? For de Sade, it ended in an insane asylum. His diaries from prison are filled with the numerological ravings of a madman. For most sex addicts, it ends in heartbreak, broken homes, or even death. Is there a way out other than through some notion of a higher power?

Charlotte Gainsbourg has said that *Nymphomaniac* is less a portrait of a female sex addict than a portrait of von Trier himself. He is clearly not a perfect person and, for that matter, neither was Tarkovsky (check out Tarkovsky's *Diaries* if you don't believe me). But what is truly great about von Trier is his radical embrace of his imperfections.

In a sense, *Nymphomaniac* represents von Trier's even deeper embrace of his character defects than what he had achieved previously. He is trying, in his own way, to transcend all forms of ego and of co-dependence. There's something heroic in this and it is arguably a necessary phase in the dialectic of enlightenment. But there's a fine line between not being co-dependent and being self-indulgent, between not playing by other people's rules and playing by the hidden rules of your own unconscious, between reinventing the form and not trying very hard.

To the extent that *Nymphomaniac* represents a self-portrait of von Trier, it is a self-portrait of a sex addict who has not fully recovered, who is still trying to hold on to the illusion of absolute freedom, who, like the Marquis, refuses to be ruled by any constraints whatsoever. But like Bob Dylan says: "It might be the Devil or it might be the Lord, but you're going to have to serve somebody." In trying to free himself from the yoke of theism, von Trier has arguably tethered himself to the yoke of his own ego. When, at the end of the film, the saint suddenly becomes a sinner and the sinner becomes a saint, and the latter kills the former, this can be seen as an allegory for a Hegelian worldview that will lead eventually to transcendence—but it is also dishearteningly facile, like the end of *Dogville*. I didn't love *Nymphomaniac*, but I will always love Lars von Trier. He makes me feel less alone in the world and I would still love to trip with him.

Talkhouse, 2014

11
GUSTIBUS NON DISPUTANDEM EST

Dear Omar,

I'm touched by your kind and thoughtful words about my work but beg to differ regarding your (mis)-reading of *The Sheik and I*.

I've always loved what Philip K. Dick used to say whenever he encountered an opposing aesthetic viewpoint, which was to quote Horace: *Gustibus Non Disputandem Est* (There's no arguing with taste).

I agree with Horace, but I also believe in argument or, rather, in the possibility of communication.

So here goes.

I'm sorry you didn't like *The Sheik and I*. But the things you criticize about it are foreign to its preoccupations and concerns. It's like judging an apple based on the criteria with which you would judge an orange. The apple will always come up short.

I agree with you that *The Sheik and I* is a flawed film, and we may even agree on what some of those flaws are. But the film doesn't share most of your aesthetic and moral concerns: "The culture is mocked, easy stereotypes of Arabs and Islamic symbols abound." What you mention is only one element of a more complex dialectic at play in the film than what your own aesthetic concerns may resonate with.

As a person of Middle Eastern descent, there would have been nothing easier (or more obvious) than to highlight the tolerant and mystical aspect of Islam, and to package the PC version of my fellow Middle Easterners for the prejudiced Westerners bombarded with Fox News distortions. But why bother? I would die of boredom.

Lao Tze wrote: "When the Tao is lost, there is goodness. When goodness is lost, there is morality. When morality is lost, there is ritual." *The Sheik and I* challenges both religious orthodoxy and the prevailing PC idea of "morality" in order to rediscover the Tao. That's what, to me, makes the film truly "envelope-pushing."

Since you talk at some length about the idea of sainthood, let's begin with that. What is a saint? I once went to a lecture by Thich Nat Hanh, the Vietnamese Buddhist monk who preaches meditation and radical non-violence. But I couldn't stand how slowly he spoke. It felt like an idea of the Tao rather than the Tao itself. If this was what sainthood looked and sounded like, I wanted no part of it.

I love Al-Ghazali. I love Rumi. I even love Sabbatai Svi, the Jewish self-proclaimed messiah who converted to Islam under threat of the sword. I especially love Nietzsche, who hated both Christianity and Buddhism for their lack of life force and preached the transvaluation of all values.

I was touched that you quote my character (the young me) in *I Am a Sex Addict* aspiring to sainthood. But it reminds me of when people quote Polonius' advice to his son Laertes in *Hamlet*: "To thine own self be true/And it must follow, as the night the day/Thou canst not then be false to any man" as if it were a quote by Shakespeare himself. But Shakespeare's attitude toward his character is deeply ambivalent and it's simplistic to conflate Polonius' arguably tone-deaf advice to Laertes with Shakespeare's own thoughts on the subject. The aspirations by my character (the young me) to be a saint were similarly simplistic and based on binary oppositions that I no longer believed in when I wrote and directed the film.

So what is a saint? I believe we're all saints waiting to be recognized. Or perhaps the very idea of a saint is already the first step on the path of error because it posits some other as a non-saint. Or perhaps the idea of morality itself is the deeper problem as it blocks access to the Tao, which is the true bronze ring of human existence.

You ended your essay with a question: "Can you remove the ego while insisting on being in the public gaze? Or would that mean stepping out of the public gaze like Al-Ghazali?"

I think your question is already part of the problem. Anyone who has ever tried it knows that stepping out of the public gaze doesn't necessarily eliminate the ego any more than being in the public gaze necessarily strengthens it. But maybe it's not a question of eliminating the ego at all but rather of finding the proper hierarchy in relationship to it and, furthermore, maybe that proper hierarchy is a perpetually moving target that requires perpetual change in order to be followed.

Internet comment responding to
"Omar Mullick (*These Birds Walk*) Talks
Caveh Zahedi's *Digging My Own Grave:
The Films of Caveh Zahedi*"
in *Talkhouse*, 2015

12
DAVID BOWIE APPEARED
TO ME AS A GOD

In 1972, when I was 12 years old, I read an article in *Time* magazine about a strange new singer-songwriter named David Bowie. There was something about the article and photo that caught my imagination and I immediately went out and bought a copy of *The Rise and Fall of Ziggy Stardust and the Spiders From Mars*, which had just come out. I loved that album and listened to it obsessively, strangely compelled by the sense of menace and transgression it exuded.

A few weeks later, I heard on the radio that David Bowie and the Spiders from Mars were going to be performing at the Santa Monica Civic Auditorium (the same concert that was bootlegged and released 20 years later as *Live Santa Monica '72*). I had never been to a rock concert before but I desperately wanted to go. Having no means of transportation, I asked my Iranian immigrant con-artist father if he could get us tickets. The show had sold out right away, but he somehow managed to track down Cherry Vanilla, Bowie's publicist at the time, and talked her into giving us VIP passes to the show.

Bowie was still in his Ziggy Stardust period, so every freak and weirdo in Los Angeles was there, decked out in Bowie-esque makeup and regalia. I was the only non-adult there. My father, as usual, cut in front of everyone else in line, insisting he and I were VIPs. Years later he would declare bankruptcy, but at that moment he seemed to me to have almost superhuman powers.

After befriending the bouncers and getting us through security, he offered to take me backstage to meet Bowie in person. I have no idea if he would actually have been able to pull off what to me sounded like the rock world equivalent of turning water into wine, but I begged him not to. Even though I loved his music, Bowie in '72 was a very scary figure, at least to my 12-year-old mind, and the last thing I wanted was to get too close to him.

When Bowie came onstage, it was as if the entire crowd immediately went into a trance. It was unlike anything I have ever experienced before or since. Every gesture Bowie made was immediately repeated by every person in the room, including me. If Bowie touched his hand to his head, we touched our hands to our heads. If he raised his arms, we raised our arms. And we didn't just raise them. We raised them ecstatically and with fervor. We were like a zombie army of zealots, hypnotized by the power that was David Bowie at that time. He was simply the most charismatic person I had ever seen in my life. It was as if he was channeling God. That Bowie concert was the closest I have ever come to a mass religious experience.

We were all worshipping at the Church of David Bowie. He was like a Baptist minister from outer space, a Dionysian pied piper leading us to experience previously unsuspected dimensions. Overnight, he became my new role model and, for the next several years, I found myself trying to talk and act like him. Along with Bob Dylan, he was the person I was always unconsciously trying to emulate during my teenage years.

Cut to 20 years later. Bowie was once again performing in L.A. (this time with Tin Machine), and I couldn't resist seeing him again. The thought of reliving the magic of that first concert-going experience was too tempting to pass up.

But the crowd was nothing like the first time. These were just your typical run-of-the- mill concertgoers. Bowie had long since gone mainstream. When the then-current inhabitant of David Bowie's body came out on stage and began to play some of the same songs he'd played 20 years earlier, I kept waiting for the spark to hit. But there was no magic anymore. No hypnosis. No hysteria. It was just a concert. The astonishing personal charisma David Bowie possessed during his Ziggy Stardust period was nowhere to be seen. I love David Bowie, the person, and I always will. But he was no longer otherworldly in the same way, and I couldn't help being disappointed.

A few years later, I was taking ayahuasca when I had a vision of God. God appeared to me in the form of David Bowie. He was in a limousine and had an entourage of beautiful people with him. He was rich, successful, and enjoying life to the fullest. And I suddenly realized my image of God had always been informed by that of Jesus—i.e. someone suffering, impoverished and scorned. This was also my image of what an artist is.

What I believe God was telling me in the form of David Bowie was that God is neither poor nor suffering. He is in the world and of the world. He is active, successful and enjoying his creation. He is full of life—not on the verge of death. And somehow, David Bowie had been chosen by my tripping mind to be the human embodiment of God. It was one of the most transformative experiences of my life. It changed the way I think about art, money, happiness, and fame. My psychedelic-fueled vision of Bowie as God became my new role model. He has been a guiding light ever since.

Talkhouse, 2016

13
CLOSE ENCOUNTERS
WITH ABBAS KIAROSTAMI

I first met Abbas Kiarostami when he was invited to
the San Francisco International Film Festival in 2000 to
receive a Lifetime Achievement Award. I was dabbling
in film journalism at the time to help pay the bills but
also to have an excuse to meet filmmakers whose work
I admired.

I had been blown away by Kiarostami's *Close-Up*,
a film I had discovered in the mid-'90s. It had resonated
so deeply with me that I wondered whether there wasn't
an Iranian gene that we both shared that caused us to have
such strikingly similar formal and metaphysical concerns
—radical self-reflexivity, blurring the line between documentary and fiction, and circular narrative structures.

It was my fascination with Kiarostami's work that
turned me on to the work of other Iranian directors who
used similar formal strategies—most notably Mohsen
Makhmalbaf and Jafar Panahi, both of whom made films
that were clearly and directly indebted to his. But I was
making similar work before ever having encountered his
(or theirs). How to explain that? I had been born in the
States, spoke virtually no Farsi, had never been part of
the Iranian-American community, and was frequently

described by other Iranians as "the least Iranian" Iranian they had ever met.

And yet, here I am making films that always seemed to me sui generis but somehow bear a striking resemblance to the work of the three greatest Iranian directors of the '90s. How to explain that?

I am convinced that there's something in the Iranian gene pool that leads to this kind of filmmaking and to these particular philosophical preoccupations. Call it the legacy of Sufi mysticism, call it a proto-postmodern philosophical tradition rooted in *One Thousand and One Nights*, call it the collective unconscious. In any case, I was struck dead in my tracks and forced to pay attention.

So when I heard that Kiarostami was coming to San Francisco to accept the award, I immediately asked *Release Print*, the now-defunct monthly once published by Film Arts Foundation, if I could interview him for the magazine, and they said yes.

We had a wonderful and deeply inspiring conversation at the end of which I gave him VHS copies of the two features I had completed at that time—*A Little Stiff* and *I Don't Hate Las Vegas Anymore*. His English wasn't great but he told me he would watch them with an interpreter and I heard through friends of friends that he did in fact watch and like both films.

A few years later, I ran into Kiarostami again at the Karlovy Vary Film Festival and proposed a video correspondence. I had already started making video letters that I had been sending back and forth to filmmaker friends but I had never had a video correspondence with a filmmaker as distinguished as Kiarostami. To my great surprise and delight, he agreed, the one caveat being that we couldn't send each other video letters through the mail—the Iranian authorities would seize, watch, and most likely confiscate anything that was mailed. Rather, he proposed, we should find people traveling to our respective cities and have them hand-deliver the video letters.

This seemed like a tall order, but also an exciting one. We shook hands on it and I offered to make the first one. This is where the trouble started. I was so in awe of Kiarostami and so wanted to impress him that the video letters I began never seemed to me good enough to send and the ideas I had that did seem good enough were way too ambitious (and expensive) to complete.

So I decided to apply for a grant, figuring that a cross-cultural video correspondence between the world's most renowned Iranian director and an Iranian-American filmmaker would be grant-worthy, especially given the political animosity between the United States and Iran.

Unfortunately, my grant application was rejected. When I received the comments from the anonymous judges, I was shocked (and upset) to learn that the reason my grant request had been rejected was because one of the judges didn't believe that a filmmaker as important as Kiarostami could possibly have agreed to correspond with a filmmaker such as myself. But instead of contacting me to ask for proof of some kind—a letter of intent from Kiarostami, for instance—they simply rejected my grant application out of skepticism.

Demoralized and busy with other projects, I never got it together to complete and send Kiarostami a video letter and our joint project died a slow but natural death. Basically, my insecurity and perfectionism killed it.

A few years later, there was a Kiarostami exhibit at the Pompidou Centre in Paris and I learned that the exhibit included a video correspondence with the great Spanish director, Victor Erice (*The Spirit of the Beehive*). I was bummed, to say the least. Victor Erice was certainly a worthy correspondent but I couldn't help kicking myself for letting such a once-in-a-lifetime opportunity slip away.

A few years later, I got to know both of Kiarostami's sons. Bahman Kiarostami had seen a bootleg copy of *I Don't Hate Las Vegas Anymore* in Iran and had become a fan. I admired his work as well so we became friends. Years later, when we were both commissioned to make films for the Sharjah Biennial and my film ended up getting banned, he offered to boycott the festival in protest. I talked him out of it but was deeply touched.

Ahmad Kiarostami lived and worked in San Francisco. I first met him at the after-party for the SF premiere of *I Am a Sex Addict*. We stayed in touch over the years and became friends as well. The last time I saw Ahmad, he told me mind-blowing behind-the-scenes stories about the making of *Close-Up*. That film is still one of my favorite movies of all time.

Talkhouse, 2016

14
THE PARADISO OF RICK ALVERSON

Someone once said (was it me?) that the true subject of classical cinema is ethics, although the same could be said of storytelling in general. To put it another way, every story is a new attempt to answer the question of how to live ethically in an unethical world. A possible corollary to this claim: if the world were ethical, there would be no need for stories. Stories are our response to the immorality that surrounds us. And so stories and immorality are two sides of the same coin. They are our poetic attempt to heal a moral rift that has taken place from time immemorial.

Bertolt Brecht once wrote: "Every day, to earn my daily bread, I go to the market where lies are bought. Hopefully I take up my place among the sellers." The pleasure of this quote lies in Brecht's refusal to moralize. Brecht knows from trying to resist it that there is no outside to this marketplace. Capitalism is all-encompassing. It is the very air we breathe. It is a similar assumption that permeates the unrelenting moral transgressions that give the films of Rick Alverson their peculiar and utterly unique vibrational frequency, their quality of a primordial cry from the deep heart of moral indignation/resignation.

The first rule of classical screenwriting is to make your protagonist likeable. Rick Alverson begins *The Comedy* by not only breaking this rule but by making his protagonist as unlikeable as possible. And paradoxically, it is the protagonist's very unlikeability that the viewer ends up identifying with. We are more unlikeable than we would like to admit, and so it is the protagonist's radical acceptance of his own amorality that ultimately endears him to us.

The second rule of classical screenwriting is to give your protagonist a clear goal with clear obstacles and a clear resolution. *The Comedy* flouts this rule too. The protagonist's only discernable goal seems to be to offend every single person he crosses paths with and the only real obstacles to his doing so are his own moral qualms which he seems to be shockingly adept at sidestepping. The film's tension comes not from any external or internal obstacles to the protagonist's goals, but rather from the moral excruciation that the film dramatizes.

Kafka once wrote: "The true way goes over a rope which is not stretched at any great height but just above the ground. It seems more designed to make people stumble than to be walked upon." Like Kafka's writings, Alverson's films point to a true way, but it is a dialectical mind-fuck that seems more designed to make people stumble than to guide them out of the various circles of Hell in which they wander. And yet, his cinema of transgression is both a direct descendent of, and a passionate response to, the cinema of ethics.

The Comedy is about an angry young hipster whose father is dying. Viewed as an allegory, the dying father could be cinema, the history of cinema, or the history of the world. Like *Hamlet*, it is the story of a son's anger at the world he has inherited and a realization of the extent to which he has been disinherited.

And like Hamlet, he makes a mess of everything. And yet, *The Comedy* evinces a comparable moral grandeur, a grappling with the deepest philosophical questions, beginning with the question of *why*? Why be moral? Why be kind? Why strive for anything at all? A film about a nihilist that many have read as a nihilistic film, *The Comedy* is, in fact, the polar opposite—a deeply ethical film that takes on nihilism by trying it on for size. It is a film that, like Hinduism's Left Hand Path To God, embraces sin as the fastest path to sainthood.

The Comedy surprises by its unexpected and continual pushing of each and every envelope. The relentlessly amoral anti-hero of the film nevertheless attains a kind of heroism through his uncompromising honesty and courage. His heroism lies in his being more honest and more courageous than we ourselves are. He represents an ideal of non-conformity to which we can only aspire despite the horror we simultaneously feel for his Nietzschean refusal to live by any moral code other than the will to power. His only moral compass is a moment-by-moment search for the action that will make him feel most alive.

Like Dante's *The Divine Comedy*, Alverson's *The Comedy* is ultimately about the struggle for redemption, for a way out of the dark woods in which we have become lost. But the simple solutions of one-size-fits-all Catholicism no longer work in the particular Hell that is contemporary America, and the path to salvation requires an individual approach in which it is necessary to leave the dictates of previously-agreed-upon social conventions far behind. It is only through his relentless transgressions that he is able to attain the vision of innocence that ends the film. Like the end of Fellini's *La Dolce Vita*, it is an innocence that is both surprising and hard won.

If *The Comedy* is Alverson's response to Dante's *Inferno*, then *Entertainment* is his *Purgatorio*. Like the *Purgatorio*, *Entertainment* is about waiting. A man is waiting to go onstage, waiting for his daughter to forgive him, and waiting to arrive in the promised land of celebrityhood. Kafka once wrote: "I am the eternal hesitation before my birth." This perpetual hesitation before his birth reaches a turning point when the protagonist comes upon a woman giving birth in a public bathroom. There is a moment's hesitation in which we are not sure if he will help her or not. The protagonist of *The Comedy* would not have. But the entertainer does, and his salvation is somehow assured from that point on, despite the fact that the baby is stillborn.

Kafka also wrote: "There are two cardinal sins from which all the others spring: impatience and laziness. Because of impatience we were driven out of Paradise, because of laziness we cannot return. Perhaps, however, there is only one cardinal sin: impatience. Because of impatience we were driven out, because of impatience we cannot return." *Entertainment* is a film about the interpenetration of patience and impatience—the impatience to be born giving birth to the patience required to give birth. Impatience, according to Maurice Blanchot (who was also Kafka-obsessed) is the deep heart of patience. The protagonist's impatience with his hecklers is the flip side of his heartbreaking patience in the face of the incomprehension with which his comedy act is received.

It is through the painstaking working out of the patience-impatience dialectic during his wandering in the desert that the film's protagonist is eventually able to enter the promised land. The comedian's final emergence from a wedding cake at the celebrity party becomes an image of his own birth. When he breaks down crying (like a baby), we know why, and under-stand the magnitude of the spiritual transformation that is taking place. His subsequent self-baptism in the swimming pool communicates to us that somehow, despite the continuing vicissitudes and humiliations of daily life, something broken has been healed.

Like *The Comedy*, *Entertainment* is a spiritually uplifting film. Indeed, what these two films share is an unblinking reconciliation of the relationship between comedy and cruelty, between entertainment and despair, between the profane and the spiritual. *Entertainment* is uplifting precisely because, like Orpheus, it descends into Hell in order to redeem life. Maurice Blanchot describes Orpheus' look backwards and his subsequent loss of Eurydice, in this case the Enter-tainer's absent daughter, not as an act of negligence on Orpheus' part, but as a precondition for the artist to have something worth saying. It is because Orpheus looks death in the face that he is a poet.

Rick Alverson's films qualify as poetry precisely because they gaze unflinchingly at the darkest recesses of the human condition. His films make no excuses for his characters and never pander to the audience. His work is unique in contemporary American cinema in its willingness to grapple with the depths of despair, its dizzying cinematic ambition, and its uncompromising portrait of the spiritual hollowness of contemporary culture.

Previously unpublished, 2016

15
DYING ON THE
MARVEL UNIVERSE ALTAR

I

Yesterday, my 10 year-old son googled the word "does." The first thing that came up was "does iron man die?" The second was "does thanos die?" The third was "does rice have gluten?"

II

Whether you like *Avengers: Endgame* or not, it is an important film. It is, at the present moment, a direct pipeline into the collective unconscious—not only is it primed to become one of the highest grossing movies of all time, it is also the final installment and apotheosis of 22 Marvel films which, given the long slow decline of the various religious myths that had previously absorbed our imaginations, now lay claim to being the closest thing to a religious myth for our troubled times.

III

Joseph Campbell, the late great scholar of myth, spoke eloquently about our deep-seated need for myths that speak to who we are today as opposed to who our ancestors were two or three thousand years ago. George Lucas famously attempted to provide such a contemporarily relevant myth when he made *Star Wars* and he certainly succeeded in striking a nerve in the cultural zeitgeist, despite his drawing-by-numbers version of myth-making: take a little Christianity, throw in some Arthurian Legend, add a dash of science fiction, and voilà. Despite its artistic limitations, *Star Wars* did somehow speak to the mythic void that is contemporary culture.

Hollywood cinema in general has been the twentieth century's closest thing to a living religion. Hollywood movie stars were our gods and we worshipped at their altars. And then somewhere in the latter part of the century, money became our god and the highest grossing film became the altar at which we began to worship.

Enter *Avengers: Endgame*. Marvel and DC have, in the twenty-first century, definitively imposed themselves as the hegemonic mythos of our time. Not just children but adults worship at their altar. The Marvel and DC universe of superheros speak not only to children whose need to project themselves as having superpowers is understandable but also adults whose need for the exact same thing is arguably alarming.

That said, *Avengers: Endgame* is, given the conventions and aesthetic assumptions of Hollywood cinema, quite good. The climactic battle between the forces of good and evil is almost Biblical in its epic scope.

When Iron Man dies at the end, it is as if Jesus died, and the myth is clearly indebted to the story of Jesus' sacrifice of his life to save us from eternal damnation.

I, personally, couldn't care less about Iron Man's death. But I found myself crying. The man in the row in front of me was sobbing uncontrollably. Others in the audience, mostly adults, were also openly weeping.

IV

I tried to cast Robert Downey Jr in a film once. Someone I knew knew someone he knew and this person agreed to give Robert Downey Jr. a copy of the script. It was right around the time he was in Hollywood jail for having been arrested for trespassing when he was found high on drugs in someone else's house. In short, he was on the Hollywood shit list and needed to be rehabilitated.

He ended up turning down the role and the reason given was that he needed to make "bigger films." He was apparently "broke" at the time, but more importantly, he needed to get his credibility back with the studio system.

A few years later, he was cast to play Iron Man, and the rest is history.

V

My wife and I had a son and my son, like most kids his age, was obsessed with superheroes. He wore leggings well past the time that it was considered socially acceptable for boys his age and he did it because superheroes wore leggings. I was always proud of his sartorial singularity but at a certain point social opprobrium overrode his love of superheroes and the leggings were never seen again.

VI

A few days before the film opened, my ex-wife informed me that the opening night screenings were quickly selling out and that I should buy tickets immediately if I wanted to provide our son with the rare and socially-prized gift of taking him to see the film on opening night, a prospect that he was clearly excited about. I was able to get tickets and my son was ecstatic. I felt like a good father.

VII

A few years ago, there was a public feud between Robert Downey Jr. and Alejandro Iñárritu. Iñárritu had said something mildly critical of superhero films—not that they lacked artistic value but that their stranglehold on the marketplace was having the unfortunate consequence of wiping out other forms of cinema which, while less popular, nevertheless have an important role to play in contemporary culture. In short, he was arguing against a monolithic film culture that worshipped solely at the box office altar.

Robert Downey Jr., who began his career acting in smaller independent films, publicly rebuked Iñárritu by saying that those other forms of cinema were dying not because the superhero films were killing them but because the films were boring and deserved to die.

I, personally, found this annoying: a multi-millionaire was attacking art cinema, a cinema he used to be involved in, by essentially making the mercenary and philistine claim that the value of art is measured by how many people like it, with no acknowledgment whatsoever of the complexities of aesthetic standards, the problem of accessibility, or the overwhelming power of the publicity machine that the Hollywood studios control. I am no huge fan of Iñárritu, who strikes me as rather Hollywood himself, but by comparison to Robert Downey Jr., he seemed like an ascetic monk with principles.

But here's the thing: Robert Downey Jr. really and truly is the greatest movie star of our time. His achievement in the Marvel films has always been impressive but his achievement in *Avengers: Endgame* is nothing short of extraordinary. He embodies the collective unconscious' projection of how we would like to see ourselves better than anyone.

VIII

I ran into Nick Dawson, the editor of *Talkhouse*, at a screening. He overheard me mention to someone that I had just seen *Avengers: Endgame* the night before. He asked me if I would be interested in writing about it, and I agreed because it occurred to me that my son might get a kick out of it.

When I told my son that I had been asked to write about *Avengers: Endgame*, he was excited. He asked if he could help me write it and I said sure. He sat down at his computer and started writing his review. He wrote for hours.

His review was pretty good! He used a couple of words incorrectly ("detrimental" instead of "distinctive"), but his reasoning was sound and his insights were, I thought, insightful. Here's an excerpt from his review:

"The fact that they had *multiple* ways of time travel took away from the feeling of dread or suspense when they do something wrong, or lose something important, because they can just go back in time and redo that mistake."

That really is arguably the biggest narrative weakness of the film.

He ended his review with:

"Thanks for reading! Oh no Thanos is snapping me out of existence!"

IX

Here's what I liked about *Avengers: Endgame:*

1. The setting up of the stakes for Iron Man in agreeing to risk losing his family in order to try to reverse Thanos' destruction of half of all human life, including half the Avengers. This narrative device was extremely effective and gave the film a certain tragic grandeur.

2. The introduction of an overweight alcoholic Thor who redeems himself in the end not by re-becoming the ripped Thor of yesteryear but by becoming the person he really is deep down when he's not acting out the public "role" of immortal protector of Asgard.

3. Thanos is not a two-dimensional bad guy. He means well and is trying to do what's right. He is a noble if misguided character. Like his daughter says of him at one point: "He's a lot of things, but dishonest is not one of them."

4. The film means well. The message that we can defeat evil if we band together, that one person alone can't defeat the forces of darkness, and that loyalty and forgiveness are cardinal virtues fits perfectly with spiritual traditions everywhere.

Here's what I didn't like about *Avengers: Endgame*:

1. It reinforces the idea that we are helpless without super powers and that we can sit back and let "heroes" do our work for us. In that sense, it encourages real-life passivity by allowing us to act out our fantasies of agency and power in a virtual way.

2. The narrative weakness involving time travel already mentioned by my ten-year old.

3. It is the perfect expression of the infantilism and immaturity of contemporary culture.

X

My son said he thought the film was too long (it lasts three hours), and that it should have ended before the "last twenty minutes," by which he meant the scene of Iron Man's funeral and of Captain America's undoing of the past in which he didn't end up with the girl. This time he ends up with the girl and lives a long and happy life of domestic bliss—the same domestic bliss that we, the audience members, tell ourselves we have chosen over our other possible future: being superheroes.

Captain America thus becomes the symbol of the compromise we have all chosen to make in order to live under capitalism, whereas Iron Man becomes the symbol of the refusal to compromise that we secretly still aspire to. But they are also best friends and the film, like most allegories, attempts to integrate these normally opposing sides of our selves.

At the end of the film, Captain America has turned into us: old, anonymous, safe. He is playing small, but he is secretly great. And his choice to prioritize love over heroism is admirable and mature.

Iron Man, on the other hand, represents everything we wish we were (and secretly believe we still are): brilliant, heroic, funny, and willing to die for what we believe in.

Captain America is no longer willing to die, and neither are we. We, who represent the majority of the country, don't take to the streets to overthrow a fascist government installed by Putin because we would rather enjoy our domestic tranquility and not risk losing the little bit of happiness we still have. Like Captain America, we are myopic and ahistorical.

Iron Man is the one who dies instead of us. We don't have to die because he enacted for us our fantasies of grandiosity and absolved us from the need to be super-heroes in real life. By acting out our super-hero fantasies in the safety of a passion play, we don't need to bear that cross ourselves.

XI

Iñárritu was right that art films attempt to grapple with the very real problems we face in our daily lives, and that this grappling is important and essential to our survival as a species. *Avengers: Endgame*, like every other movie in the Marvel universe, represents capitalism's latest attempt to subvert, commodify, and ultimately trivialize those very real problems.

But you can't really blame Marvel any more than you can blame Robert Downey Jr. He's just the spokesman for the people who write his paycheck. His attitude is neither admirable nor high-minded but it does pay the bills.

And you can't really blame the viewers who flock to these films in droves instead of taking the trouble to grapple with the uncertainties and discomforts of art cinema. They're tired, they're overworked, they're scared, and who can blame them? Their lives are hard and getting harder all the time.

All you can really do is marvel at what Marvel has created: an entire universe, filled with characters who are the contemporary equivalents of the Greek and Norse gods, played by actors who are themselves contemporary equivalents of the gods of yore, acting out the same mythological tropes that the Judeo-Christian tradition has trafficked in for thousands of years. And people are going to this church. They are attending in droves and they are making the church very rich.

It is a kind of eucharist, a partaking in the blood and body of Christ. Robert Downey Jr. is Christ, *Avengers: Endgame* is the Passion Play, and the Marvel Universe is our new religion. It's not a terrible religion, as far as religions go. But, like most religions, the case could certainly be made that it is more opiate than cure, when a cure is what we need right now.

Talkhouse, 2019

16
I LOVED D. A. PENNEBAKER

I first met D. A. Pennebaker at the Florence Film Festival in 1990. It was my first film festival ever. I was there with my first feature. He was there with *Depeche Mode 101*.

He told me he thought my film was better than *Stranger Than Paradise*, a film that was, for me, a magical work of genius that existed in some untouchable Platonic realm. For my film to be compared favorably to that sacred text was something I would never have even dared imagine. But I loved him for saying it and have loved him ever since.

I remember meeting Chris Hegedus for the first time and how I liked her right away. She was so down to earth. Once, when she was in San Francisco on her birthday, we went hiking together to the top of a hill overlooking the Castro district where I had recently shot a crucifixion scene for one of my films. During our hike, she told me the story of how she and Penny met. I remember talking with her about the likelihood, given the age difference between them, that he would die first. I also remember talking about what that would be like for her.

I saw Chris and Penny many times over the years, usually at film festivals, or when I would be in New

York, or when one or both of them would be visiting California.

Penny shot the *Ziggy Stardust and The Spiders from Mars* concert film. I was a huge Bowie fan and was always trying to get him to tell me more Bowie stories. I remember him telling me that Bowie in real life was nothing like his on-stage persona. Rather, he was super-organized and efficient—like an accountant. I also remember him telling me about the time Bowie talked him into carrying the suitcase with the drugs inside, because no one would suspect him.

When *The War Room* was nominated for an Oscar, Chris and Penny invited me to their Oscar party. One of the people who happened to be there was Victoria Williams, the country singer whose music I had been obsessed with ever since I saw her open for Harry Dean Stanton at McCabe's. Penny and Chris had made a short film about her which they had sent me. Watching the short had inspired a huge crush. But she seemed to be going out with the lead singer of The Lemonheads (who was also there), so my romantic aspirations were quickly dashed.

When *The War Room* didn't win, we were all disappointed, but Penny seemed the least disappointed. He said that he never expected to win. He was just enjoying the ride.

Penny was preternaturally young. He was in his 70s when I met him and he seemed like a man of 40. I remember thinking: "Gee, I hope I'm as alive and razor sharp in my 50s as he is in his 70s."

Penny was hard to describe. He was an utterly unique person. He was a free spirit before that term even existed. He was a role model for how to live the art life with dignity, curiosity, empathy, and joy. He was interested in absolutely everything.

A few years ago, my wife and young son and I visited Chris and Penny at their apartment. His hearing had started to go a little and it occurred to me how hard that must have been for him. He had always been such an attentive listener and such a keen interlocutor.

A few years later, I started working on a film about Timothy Leary's Millbrook experiment. During the course of my research, I discovered that Penny knew Leary and had filmed his wedding at Millbrook! I couldn't believe it. Penny sent me a copy of the film. I kept meaning to make time to ask him to tell me Timothy Leary stories, but that conversation kept getting deferred and then it was too late.

The last time I saw him was when I invited Chris and Penny to show *Unlocking the Cage* to my Contemporary Independent Cinema class. Afterwards, we decided to get a bite to eat. I suggested a restaurant a block away and we started off in that direction. But Penny was having a hard time walking (he was 92 by then) and he seemed exhausted by the effort. I felt bad for making him walk that far. There was a place much nearer we could have gone to.

As lunch was ending, I thought to myself: "I wonder if I'll ever see Penny again or if this might be it." I remember giving him an extra big hug in an "in case I never see you again" kind of way. I remember watching him and Chris walk away. I remember wondering what it would be like for Chris when Penny died.

Two nights ago, a friend posted a picture of Penny on Twitter, but I didn't understand why. And then last night, someone I work with said: "Did you hear that D. A. Pennebaker died?" I literally fell out of my chair. It was as if I had been punched. It seemed both impossible and inevitable. I was having a hard time processing it.

The person I was working with looked stunned. "I knew him," I explained.

"I'm so sorry," he said. "I didn't realize."

He felt guilty for telling me and I kept trying to reassure him that I was glad he did. I sat there a while, in shock. I tried to let in the enormity of what had just happened, but I couldn't. I was in the middle of working and there was someone else there. I felt guilty for making him wait while I processed my emotions so, after a few minutes, we went back to work.

I am not good at grieving. I don't know how to do it and my instinct is to move on as soon as possible. But I can't quite digest this one.

There will be plaudits and praises. And they will be justified. But words fail in the face of the love that Penny inspired and will continue to inspire "for as long," to quote Dylan Thomas, "as forever is."

Talkhouse, 2019

17
THERE BUT FOR THE
GRACE OF GOD GO I

I remember the first guy who played me a Silver Jews song. He was a graduate student who had invited me to speak at California College for the Arts. He was giving me a ride in his car and he played a Silver Jews song on his CD player. He also had some Will Oldham CDs on the floor. I liked the Silver Jews right away. And I couldn't help but make a lifelong metonymic connection between the Silver Jews and Will Oldham.

I had recently made a film in which I tripped with Will Oldham. It was the pilot for a would-be series called *Tripping with Caveh*. While tripping, Will had talked about Silver Jews founder Berman (they were friends) but I hadn't heard his music yet. A friend suggested I trip with Berman next but I didn't know his work well enough at that time to be motivated enough to reach out to him. In any case, every television station turned down the would-be series so the question became moot.

As I listened to his music over the years, my esteem for Berman grew. He was obviously a real poet (he is among the greatest lyricists of all time) and there was something about the sedated mix of joy and despair in the music that I couldn't help but be moved by. I especially loved the songs: "Slow Education,"

"Random Rules," "Smith and Jones Forever," "Suffering Jukebox," "Dallas," and "The Wild Kindness."

But then I watched the Silver Jews documentary and hated it. It's the only film about a band I've ever seen that made me like the band less after watching it. The film's mediocrity infected the viewer's perception of Berman. The climactic scene at the end in which Berman breaks down sobbing at the Wailing Wall struck me as forced and contrived. I couldn't help seeing it as a kind of conformity whereas everything else I had ever seen him do or say felt like the exact opposite.

After that, I avoided the Silver Jews for a while. But whenever someone would play one of their songs, I couldn't help but be seduced back.

I was sad when I heard the Silver Jews had broken up and that Berman had quit songwriting in order to devote himself exclusively to the written word. It seemed like a bad idea. And then 10 years went by.

When I heard that David Berman had killed himself, and that he had done it in Park Slope (in walking distance from where I live), it hit me harder than I expected. He was the real deal—and to think he died apparently lonely and miserable a few blocks from where I live. There but for the grace of God go I.

The scene of the breakdown at the Wailing Wall no longer seemed like conformity. It seemed like a call for help. But instead of being touched, I had turned away. Like everyone else, I started listening to him again, but my awareness of the manner of his death inflected how I now interpreted the lyrics. I discovered the new album (which I hadn't known about) and listened to it obsessively. Suddenly, everyone was talking about him and listening to his music. It upset me that he had to die for people, including me, to be motivated enough to listen more deeply to the songs.

18
REMEMBERING KEVIN RAFFERTY

I remember when Kevin Rafferty, Jayne Loader and Pierce Rafferty's documentary *The Atomic Café* came out. A found-footage film about the threat of nuclear war that was simultaneously hilarious and chilling, it was a big deal. Everyone was talking about it. I went to see it with my friends. It seemed like a film that had always existed, that needed to exist, like a Platonic form that precedes its manifestation. There was something essential about it.

Years later, I met Kevin at the Munich Film Festival. He was, to me, a legend. He was there with his wife, Paula, and his daughter, Madeleine, who was just a little girl at the time. He was attending the festival with *Blood in the Face*, his documentary on American neo-Nazis. They seemed like a fringe group, out of touch with reality. It's weird that the film is even more relevant now than it was back then.

We liked each other. We stayed in touch.

He told me about his early '90s documentary *Feed* before it came out. It featured behind-the-scenes found-footage taken from live television feeds of various presidential candidates, including Bill Clinton, during the 1992 presidential primary. I loved that film. It pulled the curtain back on what these politicians were really like (i.e. when they didn't know they were being filmed). It was irreverent and illuminating and funny all at the same time. It was the perfect antidote to the advertocracy that politics had become.

When *Harvard Beats Yale, 29-29* came out in 2008, he sent me a link. He had gone to Harvard and I had gone to Yale. Even though I hated football, I loved the film. It was essentially a talking-heads documentary that told the story of a legendary Harvard vs. Yale game that took place in 1968. It was so simple and yet so engrossing, and it said a lot about American culture.

When I moved to New York City, we met up at his favorite bar. He told me about an extremely ambitious long-form project he had been working on for years that attempted to tell the story of the 20th century using only archival footage and no narration. He had recently abandoned it after being told by the TV executives involved that they would only air it if he added narration. I was horrified that he had shelved it. I knew it was probably a masterpiece and I asked him if I could see it. In my fantasy, I would help him finish it. He half-heartedly agreed. But then we got into a stupid argument about something unrelated and harsh words were spoken and we didn't talk again for several years. And I never saw that film.

Years later, when my web series *The Show About the Show* premiered at the Metrograph, I invited him and he came. He seemed to genuinely like the film, as did the friend he came with, an attractive blonde who worked at the New School, where I also teach.

Two years ago, I decided to heal all of my relationships. I wanted to make peace with everyone I'd ever had a falling out with and Kevin was on the list. So I reached out to him. We met at a bar. He barely remembered the falling out. He was incredibly kind and sweet. I told him about my recent divorce and the ensuing loneliness and somehow the subject of his friend who worked at the New School came up. It turned out she was also single. He offered to try to set us up on a date of some kind.

A few weeks later, he called to tell me he was hosting a party and that he wanted to invite both me and his New School friend. I was excited, got dressed up, and went to the party. But his New School friend never showed up. He felt terrible about it, but I appreciated the effort. When we said goodbye, he said he wished that I liked to drink (I don't drink at all) so we could hang out more, since that was his main way of socializing with people. I couldn't know it was the last time I would ever see him, but the moment had that in-case-this-is-the-last-time-I-ever-see-you quality. It was awkward, affectionate, unspoken, tragic and humorous, all at the same time.

I hugged him, and got into the elevator. I went down to the ground floor and exited the building, processing my feelings from the night. But the main feeling was love for Kevin.

He was a great filmmaker and a completely original thinker. When I read that he had died, I wrote to Pierce Rafferty, his brother and co-director on *The Atomic Café*, to offer to help finish and put out into the world the archival film project he had told me about. Pierce wrote back to me the next day. He wrote: "I'm sorry but that project was not saved by Kevin." I will always regret not seeing it when I had the chance.

Talkhouse, 2020

19
ON MEETING MONTE HELLMAN

I first met Monte Hellman in the mid '90s. He was on the jury of a second-tier European film festival and my film *I Don't Hate Las Vegas Anymore* was in competition. I had been a huge fan of *The Shooting*, his 1966 Jack Nicholson-starring minimalist existentialist Western masterpiece. I was thrilled that he was there and even more thrilled that he was one of the jurors. The other juror I had heard of was Marco Bellochio,. My friend Irina had raved to me one night about his 1965 film *Fists in the Pocket* and, even though I had never seen it, it had acquired a semi-mythical status in my mind ever since.

The jurors had dinner together every night, but the filmmakers always sat at a separate table. I assumed that it would be ethically inappropriate to go over and tell Monte how much I loved his work. So I didn't. For an entire week, I assiduously avoided talking to one of my filmmaking idols.

I was there with my second wife (who was also my co-editor on *I Don't Hate Las Vegas Anymore*). But I was so star-struck by Monte that I was always distractedly staring in his direction during dinner instead of paying attention to the conversation at the filmmakers' table. Monte was there with his girlfriend, Emma

Webster, a beautiful British woman whom he later married and who was clearly much younger than him.

Over the course of the festival, I would occasionally notice one of the other filmmakers talking to Monte Hellman or to Marco Bellocchio or to one of the other jurors, but I always thought of this as too morally dubious to avail myself of the same opportunity. There was one Romanian filmmaker in particular who seemed to be socializing with the jurors a little too much. And then he started joining the jurors at their dinner table, while the other filmmakers and I looked on with a mixture of judgment and envy. But I didn't feel particularly threatened by it, because his film struck me as one of the least interesting at the festival and I didn't think his fraternizing with the jurors could cause them to override their own aesthetic standards to the point of overlooking the (to me) blindingly evident mediocrity of his film.

And then it was the night of the awards ceremony and the winner was announced. I couldn't believe my ears. The Romanian director had won. So I guess socializing is the key ingredient, I thought to myself, bitterly and hopelessly, given that my own social skills are remedial at best.

Following the awards ceremony, there was an afterparty and Monte and his girlfriend approached my wife and me. They told us that they had loved our film and that it was their favorite film at the festival. They explained that Monte had lobbied for it, but that Marco Bellocchio had hated it so intensely that he essentially refused to allow it to be given an award. I was shocked. Why did he hate it so much?

They told me that Bellocchio thought it was all fake and refused to believe Monte's insistence that it was a documentary and that everything in it was true. It occurred to me at that moment that if I had overridden my conscience and joined the jurors' table at any point, Bellocchio probably would have revised his opinion of the film and seen it for what it was, as opposed to the nihilistic mockumentary he was imagining it to be.

Monte and Emma also told me that although no one had loved the Romanian film, no one had hated it either. Since it was the one film that no one had strenuously objected to, it had won.

It was disheartening to get this inside peek into film festival jury politics, but I mostly felt thrilled that Monte Hellman had loved my film! I spent the rest of the evening talking excitedly with him and Emma. They both lived in L.A. (as did my wife and I) and we made plans to get together after the festival.

A few weeks later, they invited us to dinner at their home. I remember Monte telling me that he was older than Emma's parents and how awkward it had been meeting them. He also told me about his various film projects and his decades-long frustrations with the Hollywood studio system. I remember he spent a lot of time watching the movements of ants in his backyard. He was entranced and was momentarily unavailable for conversation.

There was something aristocratic about Monte. He was gracious and kind, but also somehow far away—in his own world. He was a unique person, completely unlike anyone else I have ever met. It still astonishes me that there was a brief period in American cinema history when a filmmaker as uncompromising as Monte could get his films financed and distributed through the studio system. That period is long gone.

But Monte's death is not just the death of one of the most original filmmakers of a certain era. It is also the sudden and irrevocable extinction of all the stories he could have told us about that era and what it was like to be a certain kind of filmmaker in that particular time and place. He told some of these stories to me and he told many more to others. We will remember and repeat some (but not all) of them, and keep his memory alive until the day when no one remembers us.

Talkhouse, 2021

20
ANOTHER NEW YEAR'S
RESOLUTION BITES THE DUST

Tarkovsky once said that the purpose of life is to improve ourselves spiritually until we attain perfection. I'm not sure about the perfection part but I agree with him on the "improve ourselves spiritually" part. Which is why, every year, my new year's resolution involves some form of trying to be "more spiritual."

My spiritual ambition is to become relaxed enough, present enough, receptive enough, and patient enough to enjoy each moment as if it were my last. I call this "being art." It seems to me more important than making art. And making art often gets in the way of being art.

So how to be art?

Meditation definitely helps, so I resolve each year to make time for a more regular meditation practice, although I rarely follow through with it. Also there are other ways to practice being more spiritual, such as:

Appreciating the present moment.

Spending more quality time with loved ones.

Working less.

Working with less attachment to the results.

Listening more.

Imagining that every moment is my last.

There is an ecstasy to each moment that I experience when I'm high. I've been trying my whole life to have that experience all the time, even when I'm not high. But it has proven elusive.

My New Year's Resolution is to try yet again what I fail each year to do, namely have a daily meditation practice. Even now, as I say it, I don't quite believe I'll do it, because I don't quite want to do it. I want to want to do it, but I don't want to enough to actually do it.

What would be lost? Precious minutes each day. It's absurd, but that's what my mind tells me when I'm deciding to NOT prioritize meditation.

Do I care enough? I care when I'm hurting. I care when I'm down. I care when I desperately need a meditation practice. But when things are pretty good, as they have been lately, I start to get greedy.

Perfectly Imperfect, 2022

21
13 WAYS OF LOOKING AT WALLACE STEVENS

1.
I've never liked reality. It has never conformed to my dreams or desires. It has never satisfied me. In fact, I hate it. I hate it and I resent it. Fuck reality. Reality can go fuck itself. Fuck you, Reality. Fuck you. Fuck you. Fuck you. I hope I never see you again.

2.
I love reality. Reality has given me everything I have. There's nothing that I have that does not come from reality. Reality is greater than my wildest dreams. Reality is the only thing that satisfies. Reality is everything I've ever wanted. I love reality. I love it so much. I love it more than I can comprehend. I love you, Reality. You rule. Long live Reality!

3.
I first read Wallace Stevens on an airplane. I was sitting next to my friend Jeff Nunokawa, who now teaches English at Princeton. We were both students at Yale and were on the same plane flying back to school from L.A. to New York.

We weren't close friends but we liked each other. I had met Jeff through my friend Micha, who was Jeff's freshman year roommate. Jeff had fallen in love with Micha and it made their friendship more complicated. But I've always liked Jeff. He was charming and smart and vulnerable and complicated.

Ever since moving to New York from the West Coast, I've reached out to Jeff periodically to get together. But it never happens. Once he said he was coming over for dinner but then he canceled at the last minute. I've stopped reaching out to him. But writing about Wallace Stevens, and grateful to Jeff for introducing me to him, I've been inspired to reach out again. I have no reason to believe it will result in an actual encounter (I haven't seen him in over 40 years), but it's important to keep trying. Don't give up on your fellow man. You never know. Anything could happen.

I just sent Jeff an email. It read: "Hey Jeff, want to try again?" I would never have written to him if I hadn't been asked by a total stranger to write a piece for this journal I've never heard of and that I'm being published in right now, that you who are reading this are reading right now.

I hope Jeff answers. My son is fifteen now and he is starting to think about colleges. His plan is to apply to every Ivy League school, which includes Princeton. It occurred to me that taking him to Princeton might be a good excuse to reunite with Jeff. Maybe if I ask Jeff to give us a tour of Princeton, I'll be able to see him again. Which is exciting. I would LOVE to see Jeff again.

But I digress. The poem Jeff showed me on that plane when we were both in college was "On the Road Home." It was in the, at the time, standard edition of Stevens' poems, *The Palm at the End of the Mind*. The world's greatest Stevens scholar, Harold Bloom, had written the introduction.

If I had to take only one book to a desert island and that's all I could read for the rest of my life, *The Palm at the End of the Mind* would be high on the list. It is inexhaustible and, being organized chronologically, sheds quite a bit of light on Stevens' artistic evolution. It also contains several never-previously-published poems which are among the best he ever wrote.

But getting back to reality—so Jeff and I are sitting on a plane and Jeff is reading *The Palm at the End of the Mind*. I am reading some other book, which I've since totally forgotten. And then, at a certain point, he's moved to share the poem he has just read and he asks me to read it.

It's not very long, so I read it. I like it. I can't say I understood it the way I would understand it later, but I liked it right away. It's not all that challenging to read, and it's not as abstruse as some of Stevens' other poems (particularly the longer ones from his middle, post-Harmonium period).

It begins: 'It was when I said/'There is no such thing as the truth,'/That the grapes seemed fatter. The fox ran out of his hole." I liked that. I liked that a lot. I liked Stevens' rejection of the idea of "truth." And I liked the metaphor of the grapes seeming "fatter." And I loved the way Stevens used the fox running out of his hole as a metaphor for the way letting go of truth can make you more free and wild and brave.

What I think Stevens is saying is that it is the idea of "the truth" that oppresses us, that prevents the grapes from seeming fatter than they would otherwise be. I like fat grapes. The fatter the better. At the end of "Notes Toward a Supreme Fiction," in the section titled "It Must Give Pleasure," Wallace Stevens, speaking to Reality, writes: "Fat girl, Terrestrial, my summer, my night." He calls reality "Fat Girl." For Stevens, "fat" is a compliment. It denotes reality's superabundance and uncontainability.

He goes on to write: "You... You said,/'There are many truths,/But they are not parts of a truth.'/Then the tree, at night, began to change..." This is not a monologue but a dialogue. There are two people here. The scene suddenly gets romantic. Two different ways of describing Reality, but they are not incompatible. No truth and many truths is basically the same thing. It's just looking at it from a different angle.

I'm not going to go through the whole poem, even though it's not particularly long, but I will quote the last stanza, because it's my favorite one. Stevens writes: "It was at that time, that the silence was largest/And longest, the night was roundest/The fragrance of the autumn warmest,/Closest and strongest." It's when we approach the Real that the silence becomes largest and longest. It's when we let in the reality of night that the night's roundness becomes roundest. It's when we let in the reality of Autumn that its fragrance becomes warmest, closest, and strongest.

4.

Stevens was death-obsessed from an early age. He had experienced St. John of the Cross' dark night of the soul and understood that enjoying life was the only thing worth living for. It's amazing how long it took for the reality of death to actually kill him. But like Rimbaud, a poet he idolized and referenced repeatedly, the reality of death caused him to die before he died. In that sense, he was (like Maurice Blanchot, whom he read and loved) a walking dead man.

5.

Gilles Deleuze uses the term "an event" to describe the experience of reality not conforming to your maps of it. When it's an event, you can't wrap your head around it—you can't figure it out. It resists you. That's how you know it's real. Because reality pushes back and fantasy doesn't. If it pushes back, it's reality.

6.

Philip K. Dick, who despite appearances has a lot in common with Wallace Stevens (specifically a Gnostic view of the nature of Reality), writes: "Reality is that which, after you stop believing in it, refuses to go away." In other words, it's real alright. But reality, for Stevens is dialectical, and the only way to grasp it is dialectically. It is something ineffable and evanescent. The last line of "An Ordinary Evening in New Haven" is: "It is not in the premise that reality is a solid. It may be a shade that traverses a dust, a force that traverses a shade."

For Stevens, reality is neither a solid nor the shade that something solid might cast—like the shadows on the wall in Plato's allegory of the cave. It is a force. In other words, it is energy as opposed to matter. In that sense, the solidity of matter, the solidity of reality, is an illusion. Stevens inhabits a quantum universe in which thoughts affect what one sees and thinks. He is at the center of the world and, in that moment when one surrenders to the real that exceeds us, Stevens calls reality by its real name. He writes: "I call you by name, my green, my fluent mundo. You will have stopped revolving except in crystal."

For Stevens, reality is fluent. It speaks our language, even if we refuse to understand it. It is trying to connect with us, to communicate with us. It is the whole world and it is ever-green. When you attain the real, which is to say when you finally surrender your ego, the spinning world will stop revolving. Except in crystal. It will forever revolve in crystal. But how is that possible? It's not. But neither is reality.

7.

Stevens writes: "The poem must resist the intelligence/ Almost successfully." It is this quality of resistance that Deleuze called the event. The event is resistance itself.

8.

Diane Arbus wrote: "It's what I've never seen before that I recognize." What you've never seen before is reality. Reality is what you recognize as being real, more real than your projections, more real than your ideals, more real than your most cherished beliefs. You've never seen it before because it's always new, never the same way twice.

9.

The pre-Socratic philosopher Cratylus, in response to Heraclitus, said: "You can't even step into the same river once." And then he never spoke again. That was his entire teaching, in a nutshell. He was a performance artist long before that terminology existed. Reality is not a river. A river is a thing. And reality isn't a thing. It's everything and nothing.

10.

The boxer Mike Tyson put it like this: "Everybody's got a plan… till they get punched in the face." Reality is the boxer that punches you in the face and knocks you out. Reality is bigger and stronger than you. Reality will always win out. And no one likes it when that happens. Except maybe Jesus.

11.

Wallace Stevens once wrote: "Reality is an Activity of the Most August Imagination." For Stevens, reality and the imagination are not opposites. Their relationship is dialectical and, at the end of the day, they are the same thing. He agrees with the Gnostics, who claimed that it is the imagination that creates reality and not the other way around. For Stevens, who lived in the twilight of the death of God, the imagination is another word for God, and so is reality.

12.

In "Thirteen Ways of Looking at a Blackbird," Stevens writes: "O thin men of Haddam,/Why do you imagine golden birds?/Do you not see how the blackbird/Walks around the feet/Of the women about you?" Reality is the blackbird that the thin men of Haddam fail to see, even though it's in plain sight, walking around the feet of their women. Instead, they dream of golden birds, which don't exist, and thereby prevent them from seeing the real women about them.

13.

Wallace Stevens taught me to see. He taught me to love and embrace Reality. He taught me to appreciate and inhale "the rancid rosin, burly smells/of dampened lumber, emanations blown/From warehouse doors, the gustiness of ropes…" He taught me to see "nothing that is not there and the nothing that is." No one has ever given me so much. No one has ever had such a profound and positive effect on the quality of my life. I owe him everything, and I love him more than I can ever say.

He is a towering figure in my psyche, and my esteem for him only continues to grow with each passing year. When I read his poems, which I have been reading and re-reading for over forty years, I get vertigo because he is so high, so exalted, so in conversation with God. Like the genie of "genius" in the Rimbaud poem of that name, "He has known us all and has loved us all. May we know… how to hail him and see him, and to send him away."

Because you can't live in reality. You are always approaching reality and then sending it away. And that's okay. That's what we do here on earth. Like the angel of reality in "Angel Surrounded by Paysans," Stevens could say of himself: "I am the necessary angel of earth,/Since, in my sight, you see the earth again/Cleared of its stiff and stubborn, man-locked set." The reality that Stevens affirms is not man-locked. It is not locked at all. It is wide open, which is why Stevens can ask: "There is a welcome at the door to which no one comes?"

Reality is a door with a welcome mat in front of it. But no one is knocking at the door. No one is trying to get in. Instead, we are all trying to go in the opposite direction. But I'm starting to get tired of doing that. I want to knock on the door of the angel of reality and I want to see the earth again. No poet has ever grappled with the nature of reality as deeply and as relentlessly as Wallace Stevens. In doing so, he has enriched my life to an astonishing degree. And I just want to say thank you, thank you, thank you.

Journal of Literary Philosophy, 2024

22
BEFORE I DIE

1/25/2025
5:12pm. Yung Chomsky's birthday party is tonight. I'm not really in the mood to go but it seems like it means a lot to him for some reason and I feel a certain amount of gratitude for his many kindnesses over the years, so I'm going to bite the bullet and go despite the freezing cold.

11:48pm. The party was okay. I'm always hoping I'll meet a viable romantic partner at one of these things and I never do. But it was nice to talk to Liz and Brace, and to meet Yung Chomsky's mom and brother. Brace is extraordinarily charming. Listening to him talk, I couldn't help thinking, "Wow, I wish I were that charming." He's warm and open and unpretentious in a way I'm not. I'm pretty sure I come off cold and closed off and pretentious by comparison. No wonder they have a hugely successful podcast and I don't.

One nice thing that happened was that a guy who has a podcast called *Doomscroll* told me the *Stalker* play* we performed a month ago was the best theater experience he'd ever had. That felt particularly good in

---

* I had just taught a class on Andrei Tarkovsky's film *Stalker* and, for our final project, we put on a play about the film.

the wake of one of my students saying earlier that day
that the play was "bad" and that the audience was only
pretending to like it.

1/27/2025
11:42pm. At Yung Chomsky's party, Farah* and Brace
were both saying that I should run for mayor. They
were half-kidding, but they were also half-serious. Farah
offered to run my campaign. I'm seriously considering
it.

1/28/2025
One of my 365 Videos† on Instagram now has 13
million views. Maybe I could be mayor! And the clip
from *The Imitation of Chris‡* has almost a million.
People are asking me where they can see the film. If I
could find it, I would put it on Gumroad and charge
people a dollar to watch it and hopefully finance my
Brecht film§ with that money. But I've looked everywhere and I can't find it. I wish I were more organized.

---

* Farah Marie Velten was the plus one I had invited to Yung
Chomsky's party. She plays Ashley in *The Show About the
Show*.
† I've been doing a daily year-long Instagram project in which
I upload a short video from my life everyday in chronological
order. The video in question was a completely banal home
movie moment of me as a four-year-old shooting a toy gun
while my father reads to my sister in the background.
‡ *The Imitation of Chris* was the first film I made at UCLA
film school. It won the A&E short film competition, the prize
for which was that it aired on A&E.
§ I wrote a script about Bertolt Brecht called *How To Be a
Good Person in a Bad World* that I am currently trying to
raise money to shoot.

1/29/2025

10:06pm. The amazing thing that happened today was that, after desperately scrambling for days to find a copy of *The Imitation of Chris*, Peter* reminded me that he had a VHS copy that he had taped off his television in 1987 when it aired on A&E, years before I ever met him.

Luke† posted it to Gumroad, but it only got 3 rentals. Also, it turns out that Gumroad takes the first dollar of every dollar made, so I made zero on that one, and would have made zero even if a million people had rented it.

11:34pm. Stoned. Re-read the Brecht script in anticipation of my Zoom call with Lars Eidinger‡ tomorrow. I had forgotten how good it is. Made me feel less worried about our Zoom meeting tomorrow.

11:46pm. Should I run for mayor? Maybe. My platform—honesty. I will only take $1 per person (like Gumroad). Better public transportation. A subway train every minute. A bus every minute.

But the best part of the day was that Beckett§ came over and we assembled a stationary bicycle we bought on Amazon together. It was like a real father-and-son thing to do—building something together.

---

* My friend Peter Rinaldi has a podcast called *Back to One*. He's one of the longest recurring characters in *The Show About the Show*.

† Luke Walls is one of several younger filmmakers who help out on my various film projects. Because I am technologically inept, they often help me do basic internet things like uploading content.

‡ Lars Eidinger is one of the greatest living German actors. He has appeared in films by Olivier Assayas, Claire Denis, Noah Baumbach, and Peter Greenaway.

§ Beckett is my 16-year-old son. He was named after Samuel Beckett.

1/30/2025
The conversation with Lars went about as well as it could. He was easy to talk to and seemed to like me. He says he wants to do the film. He also thinks I should play myself.

1/31/2025
11:10pm. Lars emailed me this morning. The Brecht script is looking hopeful again.

2/01/2025
I got a call from Yung Chomsky this morning. He asked me if I would be willing to write a 1,500-word essay on any topic I want for the TrueAnon newsletter. He offered to pay me. I said yes, even though I'm already ridiculously over-extended. But it's hard to say no to money.

11:51pm. Stoned. It was good to see Frank Black in concert. It was good to revisit those songs in that way. And it was maybe even good to let the children feed themselves and go to bed without me. But I miss them.

2/02/2025
9:34am. It's James Joyce's birthday. Tempted to go to the *Finnegans Wake* study group's birthday celebration brunch but I'm afraid of it being alienating. Plus, I have the kids and I'd rather spend time with them.

1:21am. Tonight's test screening of Season 3[*] was a bit rough. This season feels incendiary. The Woody Allen reference[†] was the least of my problems.

---

[*] I have been trying to finish the third season of *The Show About the Show* for the past seven years. It's finally almost done.

[†] In the new season, I cut to a shot of Woody Allen from

2/03/2025

1:13am. I like the idea of thinking through the ethical assumptions behind the attacks on the *Show* when Season 3 comes out. I like the idea of dramatizing the court of public opinion—a kind of surrealist space à la *Ulysses'* Circe chapter.

2/04/2025

1:32am. Stoned.

Dear Beckett, I love you so much. You have no idea.

Dear Scarlett,* I love you so much too. I love you both so much. I just hope you can love each other one day even a fraction of how much I love you both.

1:42am. What makes any sense? Resting when you're tired. Eating when you're hungry. Having sex when you're horny. And making art. That makes sense to me.

I'm doing a little better with my children, but I could still use a little improvement in that direction.

It was touching what Farah said about my parenting. She's right. A lot of dads treat it like babysitting.

2/05/2025

In the shower this morning, I finally had a moment to think about what to write for the TrueAnon newsletter. And I had the same idea I always have. Why not just write a journal about the two weeks I've been given to write this piece? I already have a lot of it written so how hard can it be? Plus, I have nothing to say about anything other than "this happened."

Everything You Always Wanted to Know About Sex But Were Afraid to Ask to illustrate the idea of having a court jester type of attitude. I had been worried that the Woody Allen reference might rub some people the wrong way.
* Scarlett is my 12-year old daughter.

6:45pm. In a really good mood because I just improved episode 17 of *The Show About the Show* in a significant way. A guy at the screening had suggested a solution to an editing problem I was having and I remember thinking: "What a stupid idea." But I tried it tonight and it totally worked. The episode is so much better now because of that guy's idea. And I don't even know his name or how to thank him for his contribution to the history of art.

12:48pm. Recorded a *Conversations I Want To Have Before We Both Die*[*] episode with Armen.[†] It was great to see him and to heal the rift that had come between us when, after Kathy[‡] and I broke up, he started hooking up with her. I was able to talk about it and we were able to get past it. That was very healing.

2/06/2025
6:12pm. I showed Meghan[§] the angry post-screening tweet from the ex-fan who called me "a pathetic cowardly lecherous old man who coerces young women with new age bullshit and ruins the lives of everyone around him and should honestly **** himself. great season of television though."

Meghan was visibly shaken and upset by their tweets.

Spent a lot of the day processing that parasocial hatred. I know there's going to be more of it when the

---

[*] *Conversations I Want To Have Before We Both Die* is one of several podcasts I'm currently doing.

[†] Armen Enikolopov is a good friend. He's also a neuroscientist.

[‡] Kathy Joyce is my ex-girlfriend. We were together for about two-and-a-half years and broke up a few months ago.

[§] Meghan Mullane is one of my two research assistants. The New School allows faculty to hire research assistants with New School funds.

show comes out, so it feels important, I guess, to practice being attacked. But it cast a pall over the day.

It reminds me of the Lilliputians bringing Gulliver
down to their level. It doesn't stop me but it adds a
heavier load to the load I'm already carrying, which I
guess is the point—punishment for offending someone's reductive moralism. I remember the ex-fan saying
at the screening that they had tried to kill themself in
the past. Strange to me that their first line of attack
would be to suggest that someone else kill themself.

12:19am. Scarlett learned how to play Satie's *Gymno-
pedie #1* because I told her I loved that piece. She
recorded it and was excited to play it for me.

I've been arguing in my head with that stupid
ex-fan all day. I would say it's a waste of time except
that I'm working through something. I would really
like to use this energy to write that book about art and
ethics I was commissioned to write but I don't have the
space and time. Every hour of every day is spoken for.

2/08/2025
11:10pm. I would love to make a film that cut back and
forth between the making of a film about the life of
Rimbaud and the making of a film about the life of Van
Gogh. They both died when they were thirty-seven
and they were born only a year apart. In other words,
they were exact contemporaries!

11:53pm. Teach a class on *Finnegans Wake*.

2/09/2025
9:12pm. Julia* canceled our dinner plans. That was
demoralizing. I was looking forward not only to seeing

---

* Julia Mounsey is a playwright and performance artist who
also happens to live on my block.

her but also to getting out of the apartment and doing some socializing, which I desperately need to do more of.

Starting to worry about having the *Show* ready in time for the London screenings. But I guess it's not the end of the world if I end up screening a work-in-progress. *The Sheik and I** kept changing after every festival screening.

1:44 am. Worked with Gloria† tonight. She said she had been meaning to call me because she felt bad for telling me about the ex-fan's mean tweet. I told her about what had happened since then—that I had responded to their tweet with the single word "Cowardly?"—and that the person had doubled down by saying I made them sick and that I was trying to intimidate them by asking them why they called me cowardly and that I was "pathetic" for asking that. Gloria, who's a fan of this person's work, urged me to DM the ex-fan and explain that I wasn't trying to "intimidate" them but was genuinely curious to know why they would call me "cowardly."

I DM'd the person and, under Gloria's tutelage, wrote a way kinder text than the person deserved. But Gloria did a good job talking me down from my indignation and persuading me to be gracious and generous. I offered to have a dialogue with this person if they wanted and tried to be as humanizing as possible. The person reached out to Gloria to say "Caveh's not happy with me, lol," but didn't bother to respond to my attempt to make peace.

---

* *The Sheik and I* was a film I made that had been commissioned by the Sharjah Film Festival and subsequently banned in the United Arab Emirates.
† Gloria Cook is a young filmmaker who has been helping me on various projects but mostly on the *Ulysses* adaptation.

The thing is, I guess, and this is why it was so triggering for me, that I felt unseen. I make films so I can be seen and when I remain unseen despite the films, I start to feel hopeless on an existential level. It hurts to feel unseen—at least, it hurts me—I feel hurt.

11:58am. The story of these last days is the story of my increasing closeness with Beckett. Our relationship is very strong at the moment. I love that.

2/10/2025
12:32pm. The meeting with Arian* went well. He wants to produce the film but only if I rewrite it. He doesn't like my character and wants to rethink it together from scratch. He suggested we both watch *Freaky Friday* as a point of comparison.

2:13am. Got a text message from Yung Chomsky asking me how this essay is coming along. I responded: "It's more of a journal. Is that okay?" He seemed open to the idea, but also a little concerned.

Started listening to the latest TrueAnon podcast about the latest Trump outrages. It's quite good. I really liked Brace's unapologetic anti-Trump rants. He and Liz have a really fun rapport. But I couldn't help feeling a little guilty for not being more engaged in what's happening politically. I'm glad they're doing what they're doing but I personally feel completely powerless to do anything to stem the meteoric rise of fascism that is happening right now. Would running for mayor make any difference?

2:23am. Stoned. Father, what would you have me do? Forgive me for being so resistant to reality. Help me

---

* Arian Moayed is an actor and producer that I had sent the Brecht script to. He plays Stewy on HBO's *Succession*.

to accept what is difficult for me to accept. Help me to understand your plan for me. What would you have me do? And may I have some love in my life?

2/11/2025
12:52am. Fasted all day. I usually can't even stand to miss a single meal, but eating nothing wasn't so bad.

It was nice to walk to Whole Foods with Beckett. I wish I could spend all my time with my children. That's the worst thing about being divorced—not seeing them every day.

2/12/2025
12:31pm. The colonoscopy went okay. There were no issues. I'd been worried that they would tell me that I only had a certain amount of time left to live, or that after going under, I would never wake up. Peter recently had a weird premonition in which he was convinced I had died. And as I was going under, I remember thinking: "I'm totally fine with dying. I had been worried about finishing all of my various film projects before that happens, but I really couldn't care less. If I die today, who cares. So I'll leave behind unfinished film projects. So what? I wouldn't be the first."

But then I was happy that I didn't die. And now, I just want to finish those film projects before I die for real.

TrueAnon newsletter, 2025

23
THE CAVEH ZAHEDI 100

In 2012, I was asked to compile a list of my 100 favorite films and to give a brief description of each. I wrote it quickly, off the top of my head, so there's nothing even remotely definitive about it. It's just a list of the first 100 films that came to mind on that particular day.

1. *Sherlock Jr.* (Buster Keaton, 1924). The first self-reflexive film masterpiece is so pregnant with ideas that it later gave birth to both Maya Deren's *At Land* and Woody Allen's *The Purple Rose of Cairo*.

2. *The Circus* (Charlie Chaplin, 1928). Chaplin's oft-neglected gem boasts two of the funniest scenes in his formidably funny oeuvre: him on a tightrope besieged by a congress of monkeys and in a sleeping lion's cage, trying to quiet a barking dog.

3. *Freaks* (Tod Browning, 1932). A midget who falls in love with a tall woman while his midget girlfriend watches powerlessly from the sidelines is a perfect visual correlative for wanting the impossible in this heartbreaking and utterly original blend of naturalism and horror.

4. *It's a Wonderful Life* (Frank Capra, 1946). Capra's Nietzschean affirmation of life rivals Dante's *Inferno* for the dark journey Jimmy Stewart must undertake to overcome the temptation of suicide and come to terms with life's disappointments.

5. *Bicycle Thieves* (Vittorio De Sica, 1948). This neo-realist contender for the greatest film of all time boasts a brilliantly minimalist screenplay (by Cesare Zavatinni) and the inspired casting of a non-actor whose tragedy-inflected face becomes the perfect embodiment of post-war Italy.

6. *Umberto D.* (Vittorio de Sica, 1952). The scene in which Umberto D., reduced to having to beg on the street, pretends to be checking for raindrops in order to save face is the cinema's most perfect dramatization of the complex dialectic between humility and humiliation.

7. *Tokyo Story* (Yasujiro Ozu, 1953). Wim Wenders' favorite film by the zen master of cinema builds slowly but achieves subtleties of human interaction that continue to resonate for a lifetime.

8. *Les Maîtres Fous* (Jean Rouch, 1955). This ethnographic documentary about a group of African workers who get together on weekends, kill a chicken, go into ecstatic trance, foam at the mouth, and reenact primal scenes from the collective unconscious, needs to be seen to be believed.

9. *Nights of Cabiria* (Federico Fellini, 1957). The look on Giulietta Masina's face after her trust has been betrayed once again is as unforgettable as her slowly dawning smile at the end.

10. *Vertigo* (Alfred Hitchcock, 1958). Hitchcock's greatest film transcends the crime genre to attain almost Shakespearian proportions.

11. *The 400 Blows* (François Truffaut, 1959). Truffaut takes the invaluable neo-realist lessons learned during his tutelage with André Bazin and then Roberto Rossellini, adds a dash of French panache, and voilà: the clarion call and perfect embodiment of the French New Wave.

12. *Pickpocket* (Robert Bresson, 1959). Bresson's experiment in cinematic restraint miraculously captures the high of stealing as well as its justification in this haunting adaptation of the memoirs of a real-life pickpocket.

13. *Late Autumn* (Yasujiro Ozu, 1960). Ozu's quiet story of an aging widower gently trying to persuade his dutiful daughter to get married and live her own life before it is too late is heart-breaking for the self-sacrifice expressed by all concerned.

14. *The Naked Island* (Kaneto Shindo, 1960). This wordless film about a farmer couple struggling to make ends meet on a Japanese Island uses sound to astonishing effect.

15. *Last Year at Marienbad* (Alain Resnais, 1961). Alternately maddening and sublime, there has never been another film like it. This is the film that God intended when He invented the art of cinema.

16. *La Jetée* (Chris Marker, 1962). Marker's time-travel photomontage impresses by the simultaneous brilliance of its narrative, the bold originality of its form, and the staggering economy of its means.

17. *Vivre sa vie* (Jean-Luc Godard, 1962). Godard's masterful audio-visual essay on the art of mise-en-scene takes a time out just to listen to a song on the jukebox.

18. *8½* (Federico Fellini, 1963). Has anyone ever better captured the dream state?

19. *The Fire Within* (Louis Malle, 1963). Malle's devastating adaptation of Drieu La Rochelle's novel about a man's attempts to say goodbye to the people he loves before taking his own life is plangent with inexpressible sorrow.

20. *Andrei Rublev* (Andrei Tarkovsky, 1966). The scene with the bell is so movingly sublime that even just telling the story in words invariably moves me to tears.

21. *Unsere Afrikareise* (Peter Kubelka, 1966). Several years in the making using only scissors and glue, this short masterpiece of editing density has been a huge influence on yours truly.

22. *Mouchette* (Robert Bresson, 1967). The master of understatement's weird ending, in which Mouchette's rolling game transitions effortlessly into suicide, is the ultimate lesson in how to say more by saying less.

23. *Report* (Bruce Conner, 1967). Using the Zapruder film to startling effect, Conner creates one of the cinema's most perfect blend of form and content in this experimental found footage film ostensibly about the Kennedy assassination but really about our own mortality.

24. *The Samurai* (Jean-Pierre Melville, 1967). The progenitor of the French New Wave shows the way by transmuting the B-movie crime film into metaphysical poetry.

25. *The Passion of Anna* (Ingmar Bergman, 1969). Bergman interrupts his narrative four times to interview each of the film's four main actors about the character they're playing in this bold and fascinating experiment in Brechtian self-reflexivity.

26. *Dodes'ka-den* (Akira Kurosawa, 1970). Kurosawa's heartfelt series of interconnected vignettes about the disenfranchised poor also contains an unforgettably poignant portrait of artistic potentiality unfulfilled.

27. *Husbands* (John Cassavetes, 1970). Has there ever been a more honest, more self-accepting, more loving filmmaker?

28. *The Man Who Left His Will on Film* (Nagisa Oshima, 1970). Oshima's elegiac allegory about the futility of political activism strikes an exquisite blend of clarity and enigma.

29. *Family Life* (Ken Loach, 1971). This R. D. Laing-inflected (and now largely discredited) early Seventies argument that it's our social institutions that make people crazy nevertheless resonates with heartbreaking truth.

30. *Minnie and Moskowitz* (John Cassavetes, 1971). The romantic comedy genre is turned on its head in this disarmingly honest exploration of how difficult it is for any two people to get along.

31. *Walkabout* (Nicolas Roeg, 1971). Ex-cinematographer Roeg's baroque visual style and career-long preoccupation with the themes of Freud's *Civilization and its Discontents* finds its perfect embodiment in this aboriginal culture clash road movie set in the Australian outback.

32. *Badlands* (Terrence Malick, 1973). This true crime story's mix of realism, poetry and metaphysics has never been surpassed.

33. *The Mother and the Whore* (Jean Eustache, 1973). Jean-Pierre Léaud gives his single greatest performance as Eustache's alter ego in this relentless exploration of the mother/whore complex.

34. *The Spirit of the Beehive* (Victor Erice, 1973). Erice's subtle political allegory is also one of the best films ever made about childhood's porous boundary between reality and fantasy.

35. *Céline and Julie Go Boating* (Jacques Rivette, 1974). Rivette's playful yet spooky dramatization of Nietzsche's idea of the Eternal Return successfully marries the French New Wave's cinema of everyday life with the supernatural thriller genre.

36. *A Woman Under the Influence* (John Cassavetes, 1974). Gena Rowlands gives what is arguably the greatest performance in the history of cinema in this crowning masterpiece of Cassavetes' breaking-every-rule-in-the-book career. I think this is my favorite film of all time.

37. *Kings of the Road* (Wim Wenders, 1976). Wenders' career-long obsession with lives briefly intersecting

and then going their separate ways here finds its fullest and most iconic expression.

38. *Mickey and Nicky* (Elaine May, 1976). This tour de force performance by real-life friends John Cassavetes and Peter Falk explores the unspoken complexities of male friendship with the wildly elegant precision of tightrope-walking clowns.

39. *The Devil Probably* (Robert Bresson, 1977). Bresson's indictment of environmental destruction contains one of the most brilliant endings in the history of cinema.

40. *Eraserhead* (David Lynch, 1977). Heidegger's concept of being's self-erasure finds here its perfect cinematic expression.

41. *Opening Night* (John Cassavetes, 1977). Cassavetes channels *The Exorcist* and knocks it out of the park yet again in this mystical love letter to the theater.

42. *Days of Heaven* (Terrence Malick, 1978). The Rimbaud of American Cinema brilliantly modernizes a Biblical story, swarm of locusts and all. I first saw this film while seated on the floor in the center aisle of a church, and felt that the film had been made just for me.

43. *Perceval le Gallois* (Eric Rohmer, 1978). Rohmer opens up a whole field of cinematic possibilities (still untapped) with this stunningly bold and visually sublime medieval love letter in verse.

44. *Vertical Features Remake* (Peter Greenaway, 1978). Greenaway's self-reflexive mindfuck of a film takes the

metaphysical literary tradition of Borges and Calvino and weds it to the Structuralist film genre.

45. *Hypothesis of the Stolen Painting* (Raúl Ruiz, 1979). The brilliant Chilean director's innovative adaptation of Pierre Klossowski's novel utilizes the tableau vivant to unprecedented effect.

46. *Stalker* (Andrei Tarkovsky, 1979). The cinema's most spiritually evolved director slow tracks his way through a nuclear radiation Zone where people's deepest wishes come true, even the ones they didn't know they had.

47. *The Territory* (Raúl Ruiz, 1981). Ruiz's metaphysical companion piece to Wim Wenders' *The State of Things* tells a primal story of modern-day cannibalism by way of a Godardian aesthetic that Ruiz makes entirely his own.

48. *Diaries* (Ed Pincus, 1982). Pincus's astonishingly moving diary film shows the director meeting his future wife, getting married, having children, and getting divorced. By distilling time in this way, the tragic strangeness of reality becomes visible and ultimately hits home like a sledge hammer.

49. *L'Argent* (Robert Bresson, 1983). Pessimist extraordinaire Robet Bresson's modernization of Tolstoy's *The Forged Coupon* shows him at his most austere and unflinching in the face of mankind's moral deficiencies.

50. *Standard Gauge* (Morgan Fisher, 1984) Fisher's paean to the invisible foot soldiers of cinema, projectionists, is a unique and fascinating blend of personal documentary, structuralist cinema and cinematic self-reflexivity.

51. *Blue Velvet* (David Lynch, 1986). I watched Lynch's bold and honest attempt to grapple with human sexuality the day the film opened. It was one of the most intense viewing experiences of my life as well as one of the most healing.

52. *Le Rayon Vert* (Eric Rohmer, 1986). Rohmer's study of romantic loneliness delights with its mystical surprise ending.

53. *Sherman's March* (Ross McElwee, 1986). McElwee single-handedly popularized the personal documentary genre with this subtly poetic and conceptually elegant allegory of the Civil War.

54. *Street of Crocodiles* (Stephen and Timothy Quay, 1986). The art of cinema had only rarely managed to equal the other arts—literature, music and painting—until the Brothers Quay came along.

55. *Two Friends* (Jane Campion, 1986). This formally innovative story of friendship told backwards is a poignant meditation on youthful aspirations unfulfilled.

56. *Christine* (Alan Clarke, 1987). This handheld tracking shot tour de force about an ordinary day in the life of a drug dealer unsettles both formally and thematically.

57. *Missile* (Frederick Wiseman, 1987). The master of cinema vérité's quietly observant documentary about a military school where students are taught when and how to press the button that will unleash nuclear war is chilling in its understatement.

58. *The Thin Blue Line* (Errol Morris, 1988). Morris reinvents and reinvigorates the documentary genre by adding a heaping spoonful of fiction.

59. *Chameleon Street* (Wendell Harris, 1989). Writer, director and star Wendell Harris' overlooked true story about an African-American con artist who successfully impersonated reporters, lawyers, athletes and surgeons, going so far as to perform more than 36 successful hysterectomies, becomes an eloquent treatise on the psychological costs of racism.

60. *Kitchen Sink* (Alison Maclean, 1989). This short allegory about the sex act perfectly mixes suspense, the grotesque, and the uncanny.

61. *Pièce Touchée* (Martin Arnold, 1989). Arnold's first found-footage masterpiece hypnotizes slowly and then blows one's mind.

62. *Begotten* (Elias Merhige, 1990). This mirage of a film was one of the great filmgoing experiences of my life. It invents its own cinematic language with which to communicate the ineffable.

63. *Close-Up* (Abbas Kiarostami, 1990). This perfect blend of documentary and re-enactment is the crowning achievement of the Iranian New Wave.

64. *Short of Breath* (Jay Rosenblatt, 1990). This short found-footage experimental masterpiece expresses the ineffability of grief more effectively than any narrative film I can think of.

65. *Cabeza de Vaca* (Nicolás Echeverría, 1991). This Mexican historical drama about pre-conquest Native

American mysticism is the perfect antidote to the Hollywood portrayal of "Indians."

66. *The Double Life of Veronique* (Krzysztof Kieślowski, 1991). Jean-Luc Godard once dismissed Kieślowski's aesthetic as "designer mysticism," but *The Double Life of Veronique* manages to be both irreducibly mystical and inexplicably accessible, and Godard would have done well to learn from him.

67. *Intimate Stranger* (Alan Berliner, 1991). Berliner's innovative formal strategies raise the documentary genre out of its current social issue ghetto.

68. *Van Gogh* (Maurice Pialat, 1991). This film made me rethink my prefab view of van Gogh—no easy feat—and feel like I was discovering him for the first time.

69. *Wax, or the Discovery of Television Among the Bees* (David Blair, 1991). This brilliant experimental allegory about the first Iraq war is an anti-war film that somehow manages to be utterly non-moralistic. It is so startlingly original that I was inspired to track down the filmmaker and meet him for lunch.

70. *The Story of Qiu Ju* (Zhang Yimou, 1992). Yimou's low-key masterpiece is a quietly eloquent demonstration of the folly of revenge and the necessity of forgiveness.

71. *A Tale of Winter* (Eric Rohmer, 1992). Rohmer's late-career meditation on the age-old problem of how to tell the difference between "settling" and "accepting what is" also boasts one of the great surprise endings in the history of cinema. I think about this film all the time.

72. *Thirty Two Short Films About Glenn Gould* (François Girard, 1993). The narrative of this film proves once and for all that classical Hollywood screenplay structure is only one of many effective approaches to crafting a film.

73. *Groundhog Day* (Harold Ramis, 1993). I taught a semester-long class devoted to this film, and it still held up!

74. *Naked* (Mike Leigh, 1993). Leigh's masterpiece crackles with explosive and uncontainable energy. Seeing it was like having the scales fall from my eyes.

75. *Ladybird, Ladybird* (Ken Loach, 1994). I worship Loach and love almost all of his films, but this devastating portrait of a mother trying to regain custody of her children is my personal favorite.

76. *Salaam Cinema* (Mohsen Makhmalbaf, 1995). Makhmalbaf's hilariously sadistic documentary love poem to cinema does more to undo stereotypes about contemporary Iran than any other film I can think of.

77. *Breaking the Waves* (Lars von Trier, 1996). This was perhaps the greatest viewing experience of my life. It was like watching, shot for shot, the film that I myself would have been made had I been a more accomplished and more brilliant filmmaker.

78. *Gummo* (Harmony Korine, 1997). This experimental narrative collage film is pure poetry—bold, beautiful, heart-rending, fearless.

79. *The Idiots* (Lars von Trier, 1998). The comic despair in the metaphor of one's inner idiot is very, very close to my heart.

80. *Late Marriage* (Dover Kosashvili, 2001). This Israeli masterpiece contains my favorite sex scene and helped me to understand why peace has been so elusive in the Middle East.

81. *Lilya 4-Ever* (Lukas Moodyson, 2001). Watching this film is like being kicked in the heart over and over again. I can't recommend it highly enough.

82. *Waking Life* (Richard Linklater, 2001). There has never been anything quite like this one-of-a-kind animated dream of a film.

83. *Dogville* (Lars von Trier, 2003). Replacing sets with chalk outlines on a sound stage actually works!

84. *The Five Obstructions* (Lars von Trier, Jorgen Leth, 2003). Von Trier kills off the author (and teacher), and immortalizes him at the same time.

85. *Sunset Story* (Laura Gabbert, 2003). I've never seen a film more effective at ripping away the veil of denial that all of us—including me!—are destined to grow old and die than this unflinching documentary about an old age home for leftists.

86. *Wasp* (Andrea Arnold, 2003). Arnold's short masterpiece of kitchen sink realism quietly and gradually stuns without fanfare or pyrotechnics—just the most assured use of the medium imaginable.

87. *Eternal Sunshine of the Spotless Mind* (Michel Gondry, 2004). A film this original, this brilliantly directed and this fun strikes a perfect balance between art and commerce.

88. *Primer* (Shane Carruth, 2004). This minimalist no-budget time travel film proves the axiom that it's not about how much money you have, it's about how imaginative you can be.

89. *Tropical Malady* (Apichatpong Weerasethakul, 2004). God knows what this film means, but one feels oneself in the hands of a true artist.

90. *Caché* (Michael Haneke, 2005). Haneke's riff on Lynch's *Lost Highway* puzzles and then stuns.

91. *Grizzly Man* (Werner Herzog, 2005). The scene in which Herzog listens to the audio recording of Timothy Treadwell being eaten by a bear through headphones and then advises the owner of the tape to destroy it without listening to it brilliantly demonstrates that cinema is the art of holding back.

92. *The New World* (Terrence Malick, 2005). Never have I seen a more persuasive or more unexpected depiction of what the early settlers' confrontation with Native American culture must have been like.

93. *Phantom Limb* (Jay Rosenblatt, 2005). The master of grief's found-footage meditation on the loss of a loved one plumbs even deeper than his previous work.

94. *The Puffy Chair* (Duplass Brothers, 2005). This comic exploration of romantic attachment by real-life couple Mark Duplass and Katie Aselton reminds me of the Diane Arbus quote: "It's what I've never seen before that I recognize."

95. *Red Road* (Andrea Arnold, 2006). Arnold's gutsy and unflinching exploration of surveillance and revenge at once terrifies, surprises and disarms.

96. *Synecdoche, New York* (Charlie Kaufman, 2008). The greatest screenwriter in the history of cinema directs the greatest script in the history of cinema.

97. *The Darkness of Day* (Jay Rosenblatt, 2009).Rosenblatt's emotionally harrowing exploration of suicide makes me sob every time I see it.

98. *Impaled* (Larry Clark, 2010). This short masterpiece from the otherwise mediocre feature-length omnibus film *Destricted* is hands-down my favorite documentary of all time.

99. *The Future* (Miranda July, 2011). I don't understand why July's astonishingly original meditation on love and death wasn't immediately and universally recognized as the masterpiece that it is.

100. *Life in a Day* (Kevin MacDonald, 2011). I was initially skeptical about this crowdsourced documentary edited together from 80,000 submissions and 4,500 hours of footage from 192 countries, all shot on the same day—until I saw it. Wow.

Keyframe, 2012